FOUR-STAR
DESSERTS

FOUR-STAR
DESSERTS

by

EMILY LUCHETTI

Photography by Michael Lamotte
Styling by Sara Slavin

HarperCollins*Publishers*

HarperCollins books may be purchased for educational, business, or sales promotional use. For information please write: Special Markets Department, HarperCollins Publishers, Inc., 10 East 53rd Street, New York, NY 10022.

FIRST EDITION

Designed by Michael Mabry

Library of Congress Cataloging-in-Publication Data

Luchetti, Emily, 1957–
    Four-star desserts/by Emily Luchetti;
 photography by Michael Lamotte;
 styling by Sara Slavin—1st ed.
        p.   cm.
    Includes index.
    ISBN 0-06-017315-7
    1. Desserts. I. Title.
TX773.W75   1996
641.8'6—dc20   96-10495

96 97 98 99 00 DT/RRD 10 9 8 7 6 5 4 3 2 1

CONTENTS

♦♦♦

INTRODUCTION

DESERTS FOR EMOTIONAL FULFILLMENT *It is well known that we must eat proteins, carbohydrates, and vegetables to stay alive. Those people like me who enjoy baking believe that desserts are necessary for our creative and emotional lives. A dessert can raise our spirits, celebrate an occasion, or even make an occasion. How many times have we had a chocolate chip cookie to help us through a rough day or reward us for an accomplishment? What would a birthday, holiday, or any special moment be without a favorite dessert?*

WHY I BAKE *When people ask me why I bake, they are often surprised by my answer. I bake desserts because it makes people happy to eat them. People cannot help but smile when they talk about the desserts they like. I find that the ability to enhance people's lives with good desserts is an exciting and powerful way to broaden someone's experience.*

THE POWER OF DESSERTS *Good desserts not only offer stimulation but can be a diversion as well. With the presentation of a chocolate cake, you immediately anticipate its flavors and then eagerly take a bite. For several seconds, you are focused solely on the food in front of you. All concerns and problems temporarily recede. For a moment you forget things that trouble you, whether a problem at work or the latest political scandal. Desserts may not solve the world's problems, but they do offer respite. Absorbing yourself in the preparation of a dessert is a great reliever of tension. I know a top Fortune 500 executive who bakes for relaxation after a stressful day at work. If you are short of time, you can quickly put together some cookies; if you have some time, prepare a more elaborate dessert. Preparing desserts gives you an opportunity to focus completely on the task at hand, free from distractions.*

DESSERTS AND NUTRITION *People often approach me to talk about health and nutrition. They come to me with their heads held high and announce that they do not eat* sugar anymore, as though they have tackled one of life's deadly sins. My response is to ask them how long they have had this problem and if they have considered seeing a psychiatrist. I cannot understand what they are trying to prove to themselves or to anyone else. I believe in everything in moderation, including moderation. Most of us cannot eat desserts every day of the week without noticing enlargements of certain parts of our bodies; on the other hand, we do not have to sacrifice them altogether. One of the most important contributions the new health consciousness has made is teaching us how to exercise so that we can still eat desserts and remain fit.

MY STORY *In 1979, I got my first cooking job in New York City. Like most unemployed college graduates with a degree in sociology, I read the classified ads in the* New York Times. *One ad caught my eye because it was headed "No Typing Required." I read on as the ad asked for someone interested in the culinary arts to work in an executive dining room near Wall Street. As I had always liked to cook, I thought that this would be a fun job plus pay the rent, until I found something more serious to do. As I got involved in cooking on a professional level, I realized how passionate I was about the subject. I reasoned that I should spend as much time as possible cooking, since I knew that my interest could not be satiated by cooking only in my free time. I attended the New York Restaurant School in Manhattan and then spent the next eight years working in New York, Paris, and San Francisco for small and large restaurants, a catering company, and a gourmet takeout establishment. In 1977, I decided to focus solely on the preparation of desserts. I find more freedom and creativity within the precision of baking than I ever felt in the main kitchen. Baking uses fewer ingredients than cooking, and as a result requires one to be more introspective in designing new and interesting desserts.*

MY DESSERT STYLE *My experience with cooking has given me a palate that I use* to create desserts. In baking, people often forget that the primary reason for a dessert is its great taste, and that balance of flavors is important. A chocolate torte, for example, will taste different if you serve it with an espresso custard sauce instead of a vanilla ice cream. The flavor, texture, and sweetness of the chocolate cake will be a major determining factor in what to serve with it. Over time I have developed an extensive repertoire of taste experiences that I draw on when conceiving new desserts.

I am a traditionalist when it comes to desserts in the sense that I create my desserts from classic recipes, and although I will adapt an idea and give it a new twist, I like it to stay true to the original. Often my refinements are very simple, but the impact can be substantial. All of this may seem contradictory, and therein lies the subtlety of creativity in dessert making.

DESIGNING A DESSERT *When designing a dessert, there are several things to keep in mind. As a rule, there should only be three primary flavors in the dessert. More and the flavors get muddled. With three or fewer main components, each helps accentuate the others, resulting in a dessert where the sum is greater than its parts.*

The taste and texture of desserts differ from those of entrées. Desserts are not only sweeter but are also more straightforward. Their texture is lighter and smoother than that of a main course. By the end of a meal your palate has had many different and conflicting flavors from previous courses. Desserts should be less complex in their composition, so that after eating them, your taste buds are closed off, and there is a finale to the meal.

DESSERT PRESENTATION *There are two approaches to dessert preparation: the simple or rustic approach and the extreme artistic style where desserts become an architectural forum. I believe that there should be a balance between these two styles. Desserts should look composed and visually appealing with a definite style, but I do not like to take this idea too far. Architectural desserts should be placed in a class of their own, similar to ice* carving. (Ice carving is seen as sculpture, not as edible food, even though it is created with edible ingredients.) What is created with sweet ingredients would never be attempted with fish or beef. Tell someone that you are going to turn their salmon into a swan or a miniature piece of furniture and they would think you had lost your mind! Sugar and chocolate may be easier to mold and turn into a "creation," but just because it can be produced does not mean that it should be. Desserts should not look so contrived that you feel someone had their hands all over your food while it was being arranged, or that you don't know where to begin to eat. A dessert should not be comprised of several isolated components on a plate, forcing you to taste several areas to get a sampling of the whole.

Garnishes are often added to a dessert to liven up its appearance and give it color, but unfortunately these garnishes do not always relate to the dessert itself. The addition of mint leaves, for example, should be limited to a dessert that has mint in it; mint should not be placed on every dessert that leaves the kitchen. All ingredients on a dessert plate should have a direct relationship to the flavors of the dessert.

A dessert's appearance should equal but not surpass its flavor. Do not sacrifice taste for presentation. Just as beauty is only skin-deep, a dessert needs substance to be enjoyed and appreciated. Nonetheless, your eyes anticipate the flavors of the dessert before your taste buds go to work.

BAKING AS A CULINARY ART *A Greek proverb states that the culinary art is as important as any art and is a more consistent deliverer of pleasure. Baking is an edible art. The physical existence of the product is temporary, but once it is consumed, the memory of the dish remains. Desserts can enrich and stimulate our life experiences, and over a lifetime these experiences help define who we are. Let your passion for creating and eating desserts enrich your life and the lives of the people around you.*

CHOCOLATE

♦♦♦

Chocolate was once thought to be the food of gods.
Whether or not you believe that, the reverse is certainly true.
After eating chocolate you feel godlike,
as though you can conquer enemies, lead armies, entice lovers.
Wonderful chocolate desserts can be incredibly
simple or very ornate, but all are supremely satisfying.

Mocha Baked Alaskas 13

Mocha Hazelnut Torte 15

Chocolate Zabaglione Trifle 18

Warm Bittersweet Chocolate Tartlets with Spiced Almonds 21

Dark Chocolate Sherbet with White Chocolate Sauce 22

Chocolate Malt Custards 23

Chocolate Caramel Bread Pudding 24

Three-Chocolate Brownies 25

German Chocolate Parfait 26

Babas au Rhum Filled with Chocolate Pastry Cream 29

Espresso Chocolate Chip Angel Food Cake 33

Mexican Chocolate Cream Cake 34

Chocolate Hazelnut Torte 37

Triple-Striped Chocolate Semifreddo 38

Chocolate Peanut Butter Terrine 40

Cocoa Wafers with Frozen Hazelnut Sabayon 42

Individual Chocolate Croquembouches 45

Bittersweet Chocolate Soufflé with Espresso Caramel Sauce 47

Chocolate Peppermint Brownies 48

Gateau Royale 49

Chocolate-Filled Filo Triangles 50

Chocolate Banana Fantasy 52

MOCHA BAKED ALASKAS

This classic dessert makes a startling impression and requires very little last-minute work.
Serve with Vanilla Crème Anglaise on page 232.

SERVES 8

Toasted Hazelnut Cake

⅔ cup (2 ½ ounces) hazelnuts,
    toasted and skinned

2 cups all-purpose flour

2 cups firmly packed dark brown sugar

2 teaspoons baking soda

1 teaspoon baking powder

2 large eggs

8 tablespoons (1 stick) unsalted butter,
    melted and cooled

1 cup buttermilk

1 cup freshly squeezed orange juice

8 scoops Chocolate Ice Cream (page 241)

1 cup (about 8 large) egg whites

2 cups granulated sugar

2 ½ teaspoons instant espresso

Equipment

An 11- by 16-inch baking tray with
    1-inch sides, the bottom lined
    with parchment paper

A pastry bag and a ½-inch star tip

TOASTED HAZELNUT CAKE

Preheat the oven to 350 degrees.

In a food processor, finely grind the hazelnuts with the flour.

In a medium mixing bowl combine the hazelnut mixture with the brown sugar, baking soda, and baking powder.

In a separate bowl, whisk together the eggs and the melted butter. Add the egg mixture to the dry ingredients and stir until blended. Stir in the buttermilk and orange juice. Spread the batter in the prepared baking tray.

Bake the cake until a skewer inserted into the middle comes out clean, 25 to 30 minutes. Cool the cake in the tray.

Using a 3½-inch round cutter or large glass, cut out eight 3½-inch circles. Place the cake circles several inches apart on a baking tray. (You may need to use two baking trays.)

Place a scoop of chocolate ice cream on top of each cake circle. Freeze the cake and ice cream for at least 1 hour.

Fill a medium saucepan ⅓ full of water and bring it to a low boil.

In a stainless steel bowl of an electric mixer, whisk together the egg whites and the granulated sugar until frothy. Place the bowl in the saucepan of boiling water and lightly whisk the egg white mixture until it is hot. Remove the bowl from the water and transfer it to an electric mixer.

(continued)

With the whisk attachment, whip the egg whites on medium-high speed until they are stiff and at room temperature. Fold in the instant espresso. Put the meringue into a pastry bag fitted with a ½-inch star tip.

Remove the cake and ice cream from the freezer and pipe the meringue over the ice cream, completely covering the ice cream but leaving the cake showing. Return the Alaskas to the freezer for at least 1 hour.

BAKING THE ALASKAS

Preheat the oven to 450 degrees.

Bake the Alaskas until the meringue is brown, about 5 minutes. Serve immediately.

AHEAD-OF-TIME NOTES

The baked Alaskas can be assembled a day in advance, including meringues, and stored in the freezer until you are ready to bake them.

MOCHA HAZELNUT TORTE

This recipe was designed for Chocolatier *magazine after they named me one of the top ten pastry chefs in 1994. This dessert takes a little time but the recipe is broken down into several steps and each can be done at a different time. (See "Ahead-of-Time Notes" at the end of the recipe.) The result is worth the effort. Serve with Vanilla Crème Anglaise on page 232.*

SERVES 8

Hazelnut Meringue

1 cup (4 ounces) hazelnuts,
  toasted and skinned

½ cup plus 2 tablespoons confectioners' sugar

¾ teaspoon all-purpose flour

2 large egg whites

¼ cup granulated sugar

Equipment

Two 17- by 11-inch baking pans, the
  bottom lined with parchment paper

Espresso Pastry Cream

6 large egg yolks

⅓ cup granulated sugar

Pinch of salt

2½ tablespoons cornstarch

1⅔ cups milk

1½ tablespoons unsalted butter

2 teaspoons instant espresso powder
  or fresh espresso grounds

HAZELNUT MERINGUE

Preheat the oven to 300 degrees.

Draw an 8-inch square on one of the parchment paper-lined baking trays.

In a food processor, grind the hazelnuts, confectioners' sugar, and flour. Set aside.

In an electric mixer using the whisk attachment, whip the egg whites on high speed until soft peaks form. While the machine is running, add the granulated sugar in a steady stream. Continue to whip on high speed until the whites are very stiff. Fold the ground hazelnut mixture into the whites.

Spread the hazelnut mixture evenly inside the 8-inch square drawn on the parchment paper.

Bake the meringue until it is light brown in color and dry, 35 to 40 minutes. Set aside.

ESPRESSO PASTRY CREAM

Place the egg yolks, sugar, and salt in a mixing bowl and whisk until well blended. Stir in the cornstarch.

Scald the milk in a heavy-bottomed saucepan over medium-high heat. Whisk it slowly into the egg mixture.

Put the milk and egg mixture back into the saucepan. Cook over medium-low heat, stirring constantly, making sure to scrape the bottom, until thick, about 5 minutes. Remove the saucepan

(continued)

from the heat and stir in the butter and espresso. Strain the espresso pastry cream through a medium sieve into a bowl. Cover the pastry cream with plastic wrap directly on its surface. Refrigerate until cold.

Chocolate Cake

5 ounces bittersweet chocolate, finely chopped
4 tablespoons (½ stick) unsalted butter
½ cup cake flour
1½ teaspoons baking powder
3 large eggs
3 large egg yolks
¼ cup granulated sugar
1½ teaspoons vanilla extract

CHOCOLATE CAKE

Preheat the oven to 350 degrees.

Fill a medium saucepan ⅓ full of water. Bring the water to a low boil over medium high heat.

In a medium stainless steel bowl combine the chocolate and butter. Set the bowl into the saucepan of boiling water. Make sure the bowl fits snugly in the saucepan; at the same time, the bottom of the bowl should not touch the water. The bowl mustn't be too deep nor the water level too high. Melt the chocolate and butter. Remove the bowl from the heat and stir until smooth. Set aside. (Leave the saucepan of boiling water on the stove.)

Sift together the flour and baking powder. Set aside.

Whisk together the eggs, egg yolks, and granulated sugar in a medium stainless steel bowl. Again, set the bowl into the saucepan of boiling water. Make sure the bowl fits snugly in the saucepan; at the same time, the bottom of the bowl should not touch the water. The bowl must not be too deep nor the water level too high. Whisk the egg mixture until it is very warm but not hot.

Transfer the egg mixture to the bowl of an electric mixer. With the whisk attachment, whip on high speed until very thick. Stir in the vanilla extract.

On low speed, add the reserved chocolate mixture.

Fold the reserved dry ingredients into the chocolate mixture.

Spread the batter into the second prepared pan and bake until the cake springs back lightly when touched on top, about 15 minutes. Set the cake aside to cool.

Chocolate Ganache

3 tablespoons heavy whipping cream
2 tablespoons crème fraîche
4 ounces bittersweet chocolate, finely chopped

For Assembly

1 ounce white chocolate, melted
1 ounce bittersweet chocolate, melted

CHOCOLATE GANACHE

In a small saucepan, whisk together the cream and the crème fraîche. Scald the mixture. Remove the saucepan from the heat and add the chocolate. Whisk until smooth. Set aside.

ASSEMBLY

Unmold the chocolate cake from the baking tray. Cut the cake into two 8-inch squares (leftovers can be served with ice cream). Place one square on a large flat plate. Spread half of the espresso pastry cream over one of the chocolate squares. Place the 8-inch meringue square on top of the pastry cream. Cover the meringue with the remaining pastry cream. Place the remaining piece of chocolate cake over the pastry cream. With a serrated knife gently trim the edges of the torte so all the layers are even. Spread the chocolate ganache over the top.

Drizzle the melted white and dark chocolates over the ganache and distribute decoratively with the tines of a fork.

Refrigerate the torte until firm, at least 1 hour. Let the torte sit at room temperature for 15 minutes before serving it. Cut the torte with a serrated knife, using a gentle sawing motion.

AHEAD-OF-TIME NOTES

The espresso pastry cream, hazelnut meringue, and the chocolate cake can all be made a day in advance of when you plan to serve the finished torte. The chocolate ganache should be made, and the melted white and bittersweet chocolates prepared, when you assemble the torte. The torte should be eaten within two days of being assembled. Store in the refrigerator wrapped in plastic wrap.

CHOCOLATE ZABAGLIONE TRIFLE

I am always trying to think up new and different trifle ideas, not only because their flavors are so wonderful but because they must be prepared in advance, which frees the cook on the day of the party to do other things (like take a nap!).

SERVES 8 TO 10

Chocolate Cake

1 cup all-purpose flour

¼ cup cocoa powder

2½ teaspoons baking powder

Pinch of salt

5 large eggs, separated

1¼ cups granulated sugar

⅓ cup hot water

1 teaspoon vanilla extract

Equipment

A 2½-quart bowl

An 11- by 16-inch baking tray,
   the bottom lined with parchment paper

CHOCOLATE CAKE

Preheat the oven to 350 degrees.

In a medium bowl, combine the flour, cocoa powder, baking powder, and salt. Set aside.

In the bowl of an electric mixer, whip the egg yolks and sugar on high speed until thick. Decrease to medium speed and gradually add the hot water and vanilla extract. Increase to high speed and again whip until thick.

Fold in the reserved dry ingredients.

In a clean bowl of an electric mixer, using the whisk attachment, whip the egg whites on medium speed until frothy. Increase to high speed and whip until soft peaks form. Fold the whites into the chocolate mixture in two additions.

Spread the batter evenly onto the lined baking sheet.

Bake the cake until it springs back lightly when touched in the center, about 20 minutes. Let the cake cool to room temperature in the pan. When the cake is cool, remove the cake from the pan by running a knife around the inside edge of the pan, inverting the pan, and letting the cake fall gently onto the counter. Carefully peel off the parchment paper. Using a serrated knife, cut the cake into 4 even rectangles. Slice each piece in half horizontally, making 8 pieces altogether. Set the cake aside.

Zabaglione Cream

8 large egg yolks

½ cup granulated sugar

¾ cup marsala

Pinch of salt

1½ cups heavy whipping cream

For Assembly

1½ cups espresso or strong coffee

6 ounces bittersweet chocolate

ZABAGLIONE CREAM

Fill a medium saucepan ⅓ full of water. Bring the water to a low boil.

Fill a medium bowl ⅓ full of ice water. Set aside.

In a medium stainless steel bowl, whisk together the egg yolks, sugar, marsala, and salt. Set the bowl into the saucepan of boiling water. Make sure the bowl fits snugly into the saucepan, but be sure the bottom of the bowl does not touch the water. The bowl mustn't be too deep nor the water level too high. Cook the zabaglione, whisking constantly, until it is thick. Remove the bowl from the heat and set it in the bowl of ice water. Whisk the mixture over the ice water until cool.

In a separate bowl, whisk the heavy cream until soft peaks form. Fold the cooled zabaglione mixture into the whipped cream. Refrigerate until you are ready to assemble the trifle.

ASSEMBLY

Spread about 1 cup of the zabaglione cream in the bottom of the 2½-quart bowl. Cut and fit cake pieces on top of the cream in a single layer. Brush the cake layer with about ⅓ cup of the espresso. Repeat this layering process with the remaining ingredients, finishing with zabaglione cream on the top layer.

With a vegetable peeler, shave the bittersweet chocolate over the trifle. Refrigerate for at least 6 hours before serving.

AHEAD-OF-TIME NOTES

The cake can be made a day or two in advance. The zabaglione cream should be made the day you assemble the trifle. (The finished trifle can be put together a day or two in advance.)

WARM BITTERSWEET CHOCOLATE TARTLETS WITH SPICED ALMONDS

*My sister always requests this as her birthday cake. I make a platter of these tartlets
and write "Happy Birthday" in chocolate on the rim of the platter. You can't beat the taste of warm chocolate.
(This can also be made as one 9-inch tart.)*

SERVES 6

2 ounces unsweetened chocolate, chopped

6 tablespoons (¾ stick) unsalted butter

3 large eggs

⅛ teaspoon salt

½ cup granulated sugar

1 tablespoon light corn syrup

2 tablespoons milk

½ teaspoon vanilla extract

1 teaspoon cognac or rum

⅓ cup chocolate chips

6 prebaked 4-inch tartlet shells (page 226)

4½ cups Spiced Almonds (page 205)
3 cups Whipped Cream (page 225)

Preheat the oven to 325 degrees.

Melt the chocolate and butter together in a double boiler over simmering water, making sure that the water does not touch the bottom of the pan holding the chocolate. Whisk until smooth.

In a mixing bowl, whisk together the eggs, salt, and sugar. Add the corn syrup and then the milk, vanilla extract, and cognac or rum. Mix until smooth. Stir in the melted chocolate mixture.

Divide the chocolate chips among the 6 tartlets, placing them in the bottom of each shell. Pour the chocolate mixture over the chocolate chips, filling each tartlet.

Bake the tartlets until almost completely set, 20 to 25 minutes .

Serve the tartlets warm with a dollop of the whipped cream and a sprinkling of the spiced almonds. Serve extra whipped cream and spiced almonds on the side.

AHEAD-OF-TIME NOTES

The tartlets are best served the day they are baked. They can be reheated. Store them at room temperature.

DARK CHOCOLATE SHERBET
WITH WHITE CHOCOLATE SAUCE

The contrast between the cool dark chocolate sherbet and the smooth white chocolate sauce gives this dessert a heavenly texture. Serve with Double Chocolate Biscotti (page 203).

SERVES 6

Dark Chocolate Sherbet

1¼ cups granulated sugar

2¼ cups water

1 tablespoon instant espresso

¾ cup cocoa powder

¼ cup cognac

1 cup milk

White Chocolate Sauce

1½ cups heavy whipping cream

10 ounces white chocolate, finely chopped

⅛ teaspoon vanilla extract

1 teaspoon freshly squeezed lemon juice

DARK CHOCOLATE SHERBET

In a small saucepan whisk together the sugar and 1 cup of the water. Bring the mixture to a boil over medium heat. Boil until the sugar is completely dissolved, about 1 minute.

In a large bowl, combine the sugar syrup with the remaining water, espresso, cocoa, cognac, and milk.

Refrigerate the chocolate sherbet base for several hours to overnight. Freeze in an ice cream machine according to manufacturer's instructions.

WHITE CHOCOLATE SAUCE

In a medium saucepan scald the cream over medium-high heat. Remove the saucepan from the heat and add the white chocolate. Whisk until smooth. Add the vanilla extract and lemon juice.

Refrigerate the white chocolate sauce until cold.

Serve the dark chocolate sherbet with some of the white chocolate sauce spooned over the top. Serve additional sauce in a pitcher.

AHEAD-OF-TIME NOTES

The dark chocolate sherbet and the white chocolate sauce can both be made a day in advance.

CHOCOLATE MALT CUSTARDS

When I was a child, my grandfather used to give me my daily "medicine" of malted milk balls.
This custard brings back that memory. Serve with malted milk balls on top.

SERVES 8

5 large egg yolks

⅓ cup granulated sugar

⅛ teaspoon salt

½ cup milk

1⅓ cups heavy whipping cream

1 ounce milk chocolate, finely chopped

1 ounce bittersweet chocolate, finely chopped

6 tablespoons malted milk powder

Equipment

Eight 4-ounce ramekins

A baking pan large enough to hold all the ramekins

Preheat the oven to 300 degrees.

In a mixing bowl, whisk together the egg yolks, sugar, and salt.

In a heavy-bottomed saucepan scald the milk and cream over medium heat. Whisk the milk into the egg mixture. Whisk in the chocolate. Stir in the malt powder.

Strain the chocolate malt custard base through a medium sieve. Skim any bubbles from the top. Divide the custard among the 8 ramekins.

Place the ramekins in the large baking pan. Place the baking pan on a rack in the middle of the oven. Carefully fill the baking pan with water so that the water comes halfway up the sides of the ramekins. Cover the pan tightly with aluminum foil. Bake the custards for 35 to 45 minutes. When they are done, the outside inch of the custards will be set and the middle will still "wiggle" when gently shaken.

Carefully remove the custards from the baking pan. Refrigerate until cold, at least 1 hour.

AHEAD-OF-TIME NOTES

The malt custard base can be made a day in advance.
The baked custards will keep in the refrigerator for 2 days.

CHOCOLATE CARAMEL BREAD PUDDING

The combination of chocolate and caramel is one of my favorites. This is the perfect cold-weather dessert.

SERVES 6

6 large egg yolks

4 large eggs

¼ teaspoon salt

1½ cups heavy whipping cream

3 cups milk

½ cup water

1 cup granulated sugar

6 cups chocolate cake cubes,
each about ½ inch in size (you can use
the Mexican Chocolate Cream Cake
[page 34] or any chocolate cake with a
pound cake consistency)

Equipment

2½-quart ovenproof baking dish

A baking pan large enough to hold the
baking dish

Preheat the oven to 325 degrees.

In a medium mixing bowl, lightly whisk together the egg yolks, eggs, and salt. Set aside.

In a medium saucepan, scald the cream and the milk over medium-high heat. Set aside.

In a medium saucepan, stir together the water and the sugar. Cook over medium heat until the sugar dissolves. Increase to high heat and cook the sugar until it is golden amber in color. (Do not stir after you increase the heat.) Remove the caramel from the stove and let the bubbles subside for a couple of seconds. Slowly add the cream mixture a couple of tablespoons at a time, stirring constantly. The caramel will sputter as the cream mixture is added so let the bubbles subside before adding more cream.

Whisk the caramel cream into the reserved egg mixture. Strain the caramel custard.

Place the chocolate cake pieces in the baking dish. Pour the caramel custard over the cake.

Place the ovenproof baking dish in the large baking pan. Place the baking pan on a rack in the middle of the oven. Fill the outer baking pan with water so that the water comes about halfway up the sides of the baking pan. Bake the bread pudding until a knife inserted in the middle comes out almost completely clean, 55 to 60 minutes. Serve the pudding warm.

AHEAD-OF-TIME NOTES

The cake can be made several days in advance. The custard can be made a day in advance. The finished caramel bread pudding is best eaten the day it is baked. It can be reheated.

THREE-CHOCOLATE BROWNIES

Everyone has a view about brownie consistency: cakey or fudgy. I prefer the fudgy type, without nuts.
I added three types of chocolate chunks to make up for the lack of nuts.

A 9-INCH SQUARE PAN

4 ounces unsweetened chocolate,
  finely chopped

8 tablespoons (1 stick) unsalted butter,
  softened

1½ cups granulated sugar

4 large eggs

1 teaspoon vanilla extract

2 ounces white chocolate,
  chopped into ¼-inch pieces

2 ounces bittersweet chocolate,
  chopped into ¼-inch pieces

2 ounces milk chocolate,
  chopped into ¼-inch pieces

¼ teaspoon salt

¾ cup plus 1 tablespoon all-purpose
  flour, sifted

2 tablespoons cocoa powder

Equipment

A 9-inch square pan, buttered and floured

Preheat the oven to 325 degrees.

Melt the unsweetened chocolate in a double boiler over hot water, making sure that the water does not touch the bottom of the pan holding the chocolate. Whisk until smooth.

Cream together the butter and sugar. Stir in the eggs, 2 at a time and mix just until incorporated. Stir in the melted unsweetened chocolate. Add the vanilla extract. Stir in the chopped white, bittersweet, and milk chocolate pieces. Add the salt, flour, and cocoa powder. Do not overmix.

Spread the batter into the prepared pan. Bake the brownies until almost completely set, 35 to 40 minutes. They should still be moist in the middle. (Do not overbake.)

AHEAD-OF-TIME NOTES

These brownies are best eaten the day they are made.

GERMAN CHOCOLATE PARFAIT

Generally "German chocolate" is thought of only as a cake. Here are the same flavors in a creamy variation.

Chocolate Mousse

7 ounces bittersweet chocolate, finely chopped

7 tablespoons Sugar Syrup (page 239)

4 egg yolks

⅛ teaspoon salt

2 cups heavy whipping cream

½ teaspoon vanilla extract

CHOCOLATE MOUSSE

Melt the chocolate in a double boiler over hot water, making sure that the water does not touch the bottom of the pan holding the chocolate. Whisk until smooth. Set aside.

Fill a medium saucepan ⅓ full of water. Bring the water to a boil.

In a medium stainless steel mixing bowl combine the sugar syrup, egg yolks, and salt. Whisk lightly. Set the bowl into the saucepan of boiling water. Make sure the bowl fits snugly in the saucepan; at the same time, the bottom of the bowl should not touch the water. The bowl mustn't be too deep nor the water level too high. Whisking constantly, cook the mixture until thick, about 3 minutes. Remove the bowl from the heat and fold in the melted chocolate a third at a time. Stir the chocolate mixture until it reaches room temperature.

In a medium mixing bowl whip the 2 cups cream with the vanilla extract until soft peaks form. Fold the cream, a cup at a time, into the chocolate mixture. Refrigerate the chocolate mousse until you are ready to assemble the parfaits.

(continued)

Coconut Mousse

1¼ cups shredded coconut

9 large egg yolks

¾ cup granulated sugar

¾ cup dark brown sugar

⅛ teaspoon salt

3 tablespoons cornstarch

1½ cups evaporated milk

1 teaspoon vanilla extract

1½ cups heavy whipping cream

1 cup (4 ounces) walnuts,
   toasted and coarsely chopped

COCONUT MOUSSE

Preheat the oven to 350 degrees.

Place the coconut in a single layer on a baking tray. Toast it until golden brown, about 10 minutes. (The edges will toast faster than the middle so stir the coconut every couple of minutes for even coloring.)

In a heavy-bottomed saucepan, whisk together the egg yolks, granulated sugar, brown sugar, and salt. Add the cornstarch, evaporated milk, and all but
¼ cup of the toasted coconut. Mix until well combined. Cook the mixture over medium heat, stirring constantly until thick, about five minutes, making sure to scrape the bottom of the saucepan. Strain the mousse through a medium sieve and discard the coconut. Stir in the vanilla extract. Refrigerate the coconut mousse until cold, about 1 hour.

In a mixing bowl whip the 1½ cups cream until soft peaks form. Fold the cream into the coconut mixture.

In clear parfait or wine glasses, layer the chocolate and coconut mousses, starting with the chocolate mousse and ending with the coconut mousse. Make at least two layers of each mousse per glass. Top each parfait with some of the remaining ¼ cup toasted coconut and the toasted walnuts. Refrigerate until ready to serve.

AHEAD-OF-TIME NOTES

The two mousses can be made a day in advance. Layer the parfaits the day you plan to serve them.

BABAS AU RHUM
FILLED WITH CHOCOLATE PASTRY CREAM

A baba is distinguished by the mold it is baked in—an aluminum or stainless steel cylinder shape about 2 inches deep and 1½ inches wide, with about ½ cup capacity.
If you don't have baba molds, any small ovenproof containers of the same size will work.

SERVES 6

Babas

1½ teaspoons dry yeast

2 tablespoons warm water

1½ teaspoons granulated sugar

2 tablespoons warm milk

2 large eggs

1 cup all-purpose flour

5 tablespoons very soft unsalted butter

¼ teaspoon salt

Equipment

6 individual baba molds

BABAS

Combine the yeast and the water in a medium bowl. Stir in the sugar and let stand for 10 minutes. Add the warm milk and then the eggs. Stir in the flour and beat vigorously until smooth, 2 to 3 minutes. Cover the bowl with plastic wrap and let rise until doubled, about 2 hours.

When the dough has doubled, stir in the butter and salt until the butter is completely incorporated.

Transfer the dough to a clean bowl and cover the bowl with plastic wrap. Again, let the dough rise until doubled. (It can rise overnight in the refrigerator.)

Butter the baba molds. Divide the dough among the molds, pushing the dough into the molds so that they are all about two-thirds full. (The dough is a little sticky and it is easier to work with if you coat your fingertips with some butter.) Put the baba molds on a baking tray and cover them with a saucepan or bowl, giving them enough headroom to rise over the edge of the mold. Let rise until doubled, 1 to 2 hours.

Preheat the oven to 350 degrees.

Bake the babas until light brown, 15 to 20 minutes. Remove the babas from their molds and let cool to room temperature.

(continued)

Rum Syrup

1 cup granulated sugar

¾ cup water

¼ cup dark rum

¼ cup freshly squeezed orange juice

2 teaspoons freshly squeezed lemon juice

Chocolate Pastry Cream

3 large egg yolks

2 tablespoons granulated sugar

Pinch of salt

1½ teaspoons cornstarch

1 cup milk

2 ounces bittersweet chocolate,
  finely chopped

RUM SYRUP

In a small saucepan, stir together the sugar and the water. Bring the sugar mixture to a boil. Boil until the sugar is completely dissolved, about 1 minute. Let cool. Add the rum, orange juice, and lemon juice.

CHOCOLATE PASTRY CREAM

Place the egg yolks, sugar, and salt in a mixing bowl, and whisk until well blended. Stir in the cornstarch.

In a heavy-bottomed saucepan, scald the milk over medium-high heat and whisk it slowly into the egg yolk mixture.

Transfer the milk mixture back into the saucepan and cook over medium-low heat, stirring constantly until thick, making sure to scrape the bottom of the saucepan, about 5 minutes. Remove the saucepan from the heat and whisk in the chopped chocolate.

Strain the pastry cream through a medium sieve into a bowl. Place plastic wrap directly on the surface of the cream to prevent a skin from forming as it cools. Refrigerate the pastry cream until cold.

Finishing the Dessert

5 tablespoons milk

3 cups Whipped Cream (page 225)

Make a 1½-inch hole in the bottom of each baba.

Pour the rum syrup in a 9- by 13-inch pan. Place the babas in a single layer in the pan. Let the babas soak for 15 minutes; then turn them over and soak the other side for another 15 minutes.

Place the babas hole side up. Carefully spoon 1 tablespoon of the pastry cream into each baba.

Place the remaining chocolate pastry cream in a medium bowl. Stir in 2 tablespoons of the rum syrup and the 5 tablespoons milk, making a sauce for the babas.

Spoon some of the chocolate rum sauce on the bottom of each plate. Place a baba au rhum on top of the sauce. Dollop with whipped cream.

AHEAD-OF-TIME NOTES

The babas and the chocolate pastry cream can be made a couple of days in advance. Wrap the babas tightly in plastic wrap and store at room temperature. The rum syrup should be made the day you plan to serve the babas. The babas should not be soaked more than 1 to 2 hours before serving, and should not be filled with pastry cream until then.

ESPRESSO CHOCOLATE CHIP ANGEL FOOD CAKE

Angel food cake often needs to be served with fruit or a sauce to liven it up a little.
Not this angel food cake: the espresso and chocolate chips give it enough flavor to stand on its own.
A slice of this on the run or with a cup of coffee is perfect. If you want to turn it into a fancy
dinner party dessert, serve it with the warm Hot Fudge Rum Sauce (page 231).

A 10-INCH CAKE

2 teaspoons instant espresso powder
1⅓ cups cake flour, sifted
⅛ teaspoon salt
1¾ cups (about 12 large) egg whites
1 teaspoon cream of tartar
1¾ cups granulated sugar
1½ teaspoons vanilla extract
1¼ teaspoons freshly squeezed lemon juice
¾ cup chocolate chips, coarsely chopped

Equipment
10-inch angel food cake pan, ungreased

Preheat the oven to 350 degrees.

Sift together the espresso powder, the cake flour, and the salt. Set aside.

Put the egg whites in the bowl of an electric mixer. Using the whisk attachment, whip the egg whites on medium speed until frothy. Add the cream of tartar. Increase to high speed and slowly pour in the sugar. Continue whipping until the whites are stiff but still shiny, about 3 minutes.

Reduce to low speed and add the vanilla extract and lemon juice. Add the reserved flour mixture. When the flour mixture is almost completely incorporated, remove the bowl from the machine and fold in the chocolate chips. Make sure that the chocolate chips are spread throughout the batter and that the flour is evenly mixed into the egg whites. Do not overmix.

Pour the batter into the prepared pan and cut through it a few times with a dull knife to break up any air pockets.

Bake until a skewer inserted in the middle comes out clean, 40 to 45 minutes. Invert the cake on a rack and let it cool upside down in the pan.

Unmold the cake and slice it with a serrated knife.

AHEAD-OF-TIME NOTES

The cake will keep for several days. Store wrapped in plastic wrap at room temperature.

MEXICAN CHOCOLATE CREAM CAKE

Mexican chocolate often has cinnamon in it, which adds to the complex flavor of the chocolate.
In this recipe I hollow out the center of the chocolate cake,
fill the inside with cinnamon mousse, and cover it with a chocolate glaze.

SERVES 8 TO 10

Chocolate Cake

2½ cups cake flour

2 teaspoons baking soda

¼ teaspoon salt

1½ cups cocoa powder

1 cup water

10 tablespoons (1¼ sticks) unsalted butter,
  softened

1⅓ cups granulated sugar

1⅓ cups dark brown sugar

3 large eggs

1 tablespoon vanilla extract

1¼ cups buttermilk

Equipment

A 9- by 3-inch round cake pan,
  the bottom lined with parchment paper

CHOCOLATE CAKE

Preheat the oven to 325 degrees.

Sift together the cake flour, baking soda, and salt. Set aside.

In a bowl, whisk together the cocoa powder and the water to make a thick paste. Set aside.

In the bowl of an electric mixer using the paddle attachment on medium speed, cream the butter with the granulated and brown sugars until well combined, about 3 minutes. Add the eggs, one at a time, beating well after each addition. Add the reserved cocoa paste. Beat until smooth.

In a small bowl, add the vanilla to the buttermilk. On low speed, alternately add the reserved dry ingredients and the buttermilk to the butter mixture.

Spread the batter in the prepared cake pan. Bake until a skewer inserted in the middle has a wet crumb, about 1 hour and 20 minutes. Let cool to room temperature in the pan.

Unmold the cake on a cake rack and invert it so it is right side up. Using a serrated knife and gentle sawing motions, cut off the top ½ inch of the cake horizontally in one piece. Slide the top of the cake onto a plate and set it aside. Again with a serrated knife, cut and scoop out the center of the remaining cake, leaving a ¾-inch layer of cake on the bottom and all around the sides. (Leftover cake pieces can be frozen and used in the Chocolate Caramel Bread Pudding on page 24.) Set the cake aside.

Cinnamon Mousse

1 teaspoon powdered gelatin

1 tablespoon cold water

½ cup Sugar Syrup (page 239)

8 large egg yolks

1 teaspoon ground cinnamon

Pinch of salt

1½ cups mascarpone

CINNAMON MOUSSE

Stir the gelatin into the cold water in a small saucepan. Let sit for 5 minutes. Warm over low heat until the gelatin is completely dissolved, and set aside.

Fill a medium saucepan ⅓ full of water and bring the water to a low boil.

In a medium stainless steel bowl, whisk together the sugar syrup, egg yolks, cinnamon, and salt. Set the bowl into the saucepan of boiling water. Make sure the bowl fits snugly in the saucepan; at the same time, the bottom of the bowl should not touch the water. The bowl mustn't be too deep nor the water level too high. Whisk the mixture constantly until thick, about 3 minutes. Remove the bowl from the heat and whisk in the gelatin.

Transfer the egg yolk mixture to the bowl of an electric mixer. Using the whisk attachment, whip on medium speed until room temperature, about 2 minutes.

Reduce to medium-low speed and add the mascarpone, a couple of tablespoons at a time. Mix until smooth.

Fill the hollowed-out chocolate cake with the cinnamon mousse. Spread a thin layer of the cinnamon mousse around the top edge of the cake. Place the reserved piece of chocolate cake on top of the cinnamon mousse. (The thin layer of cinnamon mousse will help the top piece of cake stick to the filled bottom layer of the cake.)

(continued)

Chocolate Glaze

7 ounces bittersweet chocolate, chopped
8 tablespoons (1 stick) unsalted butter

CHOCOLATE GLAZE

Melt the chocolate and the butter in a double boiler over hot water, making sure that the water does not touch the bottom of the pan holding the chocolate. Whisk until smooth. Let the glaze cool and thicken slightly. Spread it evenly over the top and sides of the cake.

Refrigerate the chocolate cake until the cinnamon mousse and the chocolate glaze are completely set, 2 to 3 hours. (After the glaze is partially set you can draw a decorative pattern on the top with the tines of a fork.)

Remove the cake from the refrigerator half an hour before you plan to serve it.

AHEAD-OF-TIME NOTES

The cake can be made a day in advance.

CHOCOLATE HAZELNUT TORTE

Every baker should have a cake like this in his or her repertoire. Serve with Cappuccino Ice Cream (page 241).

SERVES 8 TO 10

Cake

1¼ cups (5 ounces) hazelnuts,
  toasted and skinned

¼ cup cake flour

12 tablespoons (1½ sticks) unsalted butter

6 ounces bittersweet chocolate, finely chopped

4 large eggs, separated

1⅓ cups granulated sugar

¼ teaspoon salt

1½ teaspoons finely chopped orange zest

Chocolate Glaze

6 tablespoons heavy whipping cream

6 ounces bittersweet chocolate, finely chopped

1½ tablespoons light corn syrup

1 tablespoon hazelnut liqueur

½ tablespoon Grand Marnier

Equipment

A 9- by 3-inch-deep cake pan, the bottom
  lined with parchment paper

CAKE

Preheat the oven to 325 degrees.

In a food processor, finely grind 1 cup of the hazelnuts with the cake flour. Set aside.

Melt the butter and the chocolate in a double boiler over hot water, making sure that the water does not touch the bottom of the pan holding the chocolate. Whisk until smooth.

In the bowl of an electric mixer, whip the egg yolks, ⅔ cup of the sugar, and the salt on high speed until thick. Reduce to low speed and add the melted chocolate and butter. Add the ground hazelnut mixture and the orange zest.

In a clean bowl, whip the egg whites until soft peaks form. Continuing to whip, add the remaining ⅔ cup sugar in a steady stream. Whip until the sugar is completely dissolved and the egg whites are stiff.

Gently fold the egg whites into the batter in two batches. Spread the batter into the prepared cake pan.

Bake the torte until a skewer inserted in the middle comes out clean, 45 to 50 minutes. Cool to room temperature and then unmold.

CHOCOLATE GLAZE

Scald the cream. Remove the pan from the stove and stir in the chocolate. Whisk in the corn syrup, hazelnut liqueur, and Grand Marnier. Set the glaze aside to thicken slightly, 20 to 30 minutes. Evenly spread the glaze over the top and sides of the cake. Garnish with the remaining ¼ cup of hazelnuts.

AHEAD-OF-TIME NOTES

The torte can be made a day in advance. Store at room temperature.

TRIPLE-STRIPED CHOCOLATE SEMIFREDDO

Here, one mousse is divided into thirds and each third is flavored with a different kind of chocolate. The three mousses are stacked one on top of the other, giving the dessert a striped appearance. Serve this with Chocolate Caramel Sauce (page 230).

SERVES 6 TO 8

Mousse Base

5 large egg yolks

3 tablespoons granulated sugar

Pinch of salt

1½ cups milk

1 teaspoon vanilla extract

Equipment

An 8-inch square pan, lined with plastic wrap

Dark Chocolate Layer

2½ ounces bittersweet chocolate, finely chopped

½ cup mousse base

½ cup heavy whipping cream

1 tablespoon granulated sugar

MOUSSE BASE

Whisk together the egg yolks, sugar, and salt in a medium stainless steel bowl. Set aside.

Fill a medium saucepan ⅓ full of water. Bring the water to a low boil.

In a medium heavy-bottomed saucepan, scald the milk over medium-high heat. Whisk the milk slowly into the egg yolk and sugar mixture. Set the bowl into the saucepan of boiling water. Make sure the bowl fits snugly in the saucepan; at the same time, the bottom of the bowl should not touch the water. The bowl mustn't be too deep nor the water level too high. Cook the milk mixture, stirring constantly, making sure to scrape the bottom of the bowl, until it has thickened slightly, 3 to 5 minutes. Stir in the vanilla extract. Strain the mousse base into a clean bowl through a medium sieve. Refrigerate until cold.

DARK CHOCOLATE MOUSSE

Melt the bittersweet chocolate in a double boiler over hot water, making sure that the water does not touch the bottom of the pan holding the chocolate. Whisk until smooth. Slowly whisk ½ cup of the cold mousse base into the chocolate. Cool.

In a small bowl, whip the heavy cream and sugar until soft peaks form. Fold the cream into the chocolate mixture.

Pour the dark chocolate mousse into the prepared pan and freeze.

White Chocolate Layer

7 ½ ounces white chocolate, finely chopped

½ cup mousse base

½ cup heavy whipping cream

1 tablespoon granulated sugar

Milk Chocolate Layer

3 ounces milk chocolate, finely chopped

½ cup mousse base

½ cup heavy whipping cream

1 tablespoon granulated sugar

WHITE AND MILK CHOCOLATE MOUSSES

Prepare the white and milk chocolate mousses separately in the same manner as the dark chocolate mousse, substituting the white or milk chocolate as required. Refrigerate the white and milk chocolate mousses.

When the dark chocolate mousse is firm to the touch (about ½ hour after putting it in the freezer), spread the white chocolate mousse on top. When the white chocolate mousse is firm to the touch, about 45 minutes after putting it in the freezer, spread the milk chocolate mousse over the white chocolate mousse.

Freeze the semifreddo until hard, at least 4 hours. Unmold the semifreddo and remove the plastic wrap. Cut into pieces and serve.

AHEAD-OF-TIME NOTES

The semifreddo can be made 1 to 2 days in advance. Store wrapped in plastic wrap.

CHOCOLATE PEANUT BUTTER TERRINE

The garnish of the sugared peanuts gives this terrine texture and even more of a peanut flavor.

SERVES 6

Terrine

11 ounces bittersweet chocolate,
  finely chopped

2 tablespoons unsalted butter

6 tablespoons smooth peanut butter

4 large egg yolks

¼ cup granulated sugar

1¾ cups heavy whipping cream

Glaze

4 ounces bittersweet chocolate, finely chopped

5 tablespoons unsalted butter

2 teaspoons light corn syrup

1 cup Sugared Peanuts (page 216)

Equipment

A 9½- by 4- by 3-inch loaf pan lined
  with plastic wrap

TERRINE

Fill a medium saucepan ⅓ full of water and bring it to a low boil.

Combine the chocolate, butter, and peanut butter in a stainless steel bowl. Place the bowl on top of the saucepan of water, making sure that the water doesn't touch the bottom of the bowl. Melt the mixture. Whisk until smooth. Set the bowl aside, but keep the saucepan of water hot on the stove.

Place the egg yolks and 2 tablespoons of the sugar in a stainless steel bowl and whisk until combined. Put the bowl on top of the saucepan of hot water, making sure the water doesn't touch the bottom of the bowl. Whisk the mixture until thick. Remove the bowl from the heat. In three separate additions, stir in the reserved chocolate mixture.

Whip the cream with the remaining sugar until soft peaks form. In three additions, fold the cream into the chocolate mixture. Spread the terrine into the pan. Tap on the counter to get rid of bubbles. Refrigerate until firm, at least 2 hours, and then unmold.

CHOCOLATE GLAZE

Melt the chocolate, butter, and corn syrup in a double boiler over hot water, making sure that the water does not touch the pan holding the chocolate. Whisk until smooth. Spread the glaze over the terrine. Refrigerate until firm.

Garnish the terrine with the sugared peanuts. Slice with a hot dry knife.

AHEAD-OF-TIME NOTES

The terrine can be made 2 days in advance. Refrigerate until ready to serve.

COCOA WAFERS
WITH FROZEN HAZELNUT SABAYON

Using cocoa powder is a nice light way to incorporate the flavor of chocolate in a dessert.

SERVES 6

Cocoa Wafers

5 tablespoons all-purpose flour

¼ cup cocoa powder

2 large egg whites

½ cup granulated sugar

6 tablespoons (¾ stick) unsalted butter, melted

½ teaspoon vanilla extract

Equipment

Two 17- by 11-inch baking trays, the bottoms lined with parchment paper

COCOA WAFERS

Preheat the oven to 350 degrees.

Sift together the flour and cocoa powder. Set aside.

In a medium bowl, lightly whisk the egg whites until frothy. Whisk in the sugar and then the melted butter and vanilla extract. Add the flour mixture and whisk until smooth.

Using the back of a spoon, for each wafer spread out ½ tablespoon of the cocoa batter in a 3-inch circle onto one of the prepared baking sheets. Place as many wafers as you can on a baking sheet, leaving an inch between the wafers. Bake the wafers until they are no longer shiny, 6 to 8 minutes. Let the wafers cool and then remove them from the trays, using a thin metal spatula. (The wafers are fragile and will break easily.) Continue baking the wafers until all the batter is used. There will be enough batter for 18 wafers plus extra in case some break.

Hazelnut Sabayon

8 large egg yolks

½ cup granulated sugar

Pinch of salt

¼ cup freshly squeezed orange juice

½ cup Frangelico (hazelnut liqueur)

1 cup heavy whipping cream

Finishing the Dessert

1 tablespoon confectioners' sugar

¾ cup (3 ounces) hazelnuts, toasted, skinned, and coarsely chopped

1½ cups Chocolate Caramel Sauce (page 230)

HAZELNUT SABAYON

Fill a medium-large bowl ⅓ full of ice water. Set it aside.

Fill a medium saucepan ⅓ full of water. Bring the water to a low boil.

In a medium stainless steel bowl, whisk together the egg yolks, sugar, and salt. Add the orange juice and Frangelico. Set the bowl into the saucepan of boiling water. Make sure the bowl fits snugly in the saucepan; at the same time, the bottom of the bowl should not touch the water. The bowl mustn't be too deep nor the water level too high. Cook the sabayon, whisking constantly until thick, about 3 minutes. Place the bowl of sabayon in the bowl of ice water and whisk until cool.

In a medium bowl, whip the cream until soft peaks form. Fold the cream into the cooled sabayon mixture. Freeze the sabayon for at least 2 hours or until you are ready to serve the wafers.

FINISHING

Place a cocoa wafer on each plate. Spoon some hazelnut sabayon in the middle of the wafer. Add a second wafer and more sabayon. Repeat this layering process another time, gently placing the wafers and sabayon on top. Dust the top of the wafers with the confectioners' sugar. Sprinkle the chopped hazelnuts on each plate and drizzle some of the chocolate caramel sauce around the stacked wafers. Serve immediately.

AHEAD-OF-TIME NOTES

The cocoa wafers can be made ahead and wrapped airtight to keep them crisp. If they get soggy on the second day, just pop them in a 350-degree oven for a couple of minutes to recrisp them. The sabayon can be made a day or two ahead of time. The dessert should be assembled just before serving.

INDIVIDUAL CHOCOLATE CROQUEMBOUCHES

*Traditionally croquembouches, tall towers of little profiteroles, are served at Christmastime
in the United States and at weddings in Europe. Here I have made mini croquembouches so that each person
gets his or her own individual tower. Serve with Vanilla Crème Anglaise (page 232).*

SERVES 6

Chocolate Profiteroles

1 cup water

4 tablespoons (½ stick) unsalted butter

⅛ teaspoon salt

2 teaspoons granulated sugar

1 cup all-purpose flour

1½ tablespoons cocoa powder

4 large eggs

Equipment

A pastry bag and ¼- and ½-inch tips

Two 17- by 11-inch baking trays,
   the bottoms lined with parchment paper

CHOCOLATE PROFITEROLES

Preheat the oven to 400 degrees.

Combine the water, butter, salt, and sugar in a
heavy-bottomed saucepan. Bring the mixture to
a boil over medium heat, and remove the saucepan
from the heat. Stir in the flour and cocoa powder,
mixing well. Return the saucepan to the stove
and cook, stirring constantly, until the mixture
comes away cleanly from the sides of the saucepan,
about 1 minute.

Place the dough in the bowl of an electric mixer
and let it cool for 2 to 3 minutes. With the paddle
attachment, begin beating the dough on medium
speed. Add the eggs one at a time, beating well
after each addition. Beat the mixture until smooth
and elastic, 2 to 3 minutes.

Place the mixture in the pastry bag fitted with the
½-inch tip. Pipe out at least 48 balls, each about
1 inch high and 1 inch wide, onto the parchment-
lined baking sheets. Press the top of each profiterole
with a wet finger to eliminate any points.

Bake for 15 minutes. Decrease the oven temperature
to 350. Continue to bake until golden brown and
firm to the touch, about 15 minutes.

(continued)

White Chocolate Cream

1 cup heavy whipping cream

1 pound white chocolate, finely chopped

For Assembly

6 ounces white chocolate, finely chopped

3 ounces bittersweet chocolate, finely chopped

WHITE CHOCOLATE CREAM

In a heavy-bottomed saucepan, bring the cream to a boil over medium-high heat. Remove the pan from the heat and add the white chocolate. Whisk until smooth. Refrigerate until cold and thick.

With a sharp knife make a small slit in the side of each profiterole. Put the white chocolate cream in a clean pastry bag, fitted with the ¼-inch tip. Pipe about 2 teaspoons of the white chocolate cream into each of the profiteroles.

ASSEMBLY

Melt the white chocolate in a double boiler over hot water, making sure that the water does not touch the bottom of the pan holding the chocolate. Whisk until smooth.

Dip the tops of the profiteroles in the white chocolate. Refrigerate until set.

Melt the bittersweet chocolate in a double boiler over hot water, making sure that the water does not touch the bottom of the pan holding the chocolate. Whisk until smooth. Cool to room temperature.

Dip the top of 24 profiteroles in the dark chocolate, making sure not to completely cover the white chocolate. Place 4 profiteroles close together on each of 6 plates. Dip the bottoms of 3 more profiteroles per serving in the dark chocolate and arrange them on top of the already plated profiteroles. Dip the bottoms of 6 more profiteroles in the dark chocolate and place one on top of each "tower."

AHEAD-OF-TIME NOTES

The profiteroles and the white chocolate cream can be made a day in advance. Store the profiteroles in an airtight container at room temperature. (If the profiteroles get soggy before you fill them, recrisp in a preheated 300-degree oven for 5 minutes. They will crisp more as they cool.) The croquembouches are best eaten the day they are assembled. Refrigerate until you are ready to serve them.

BITTERSWEET CHOCOLATE SOUFFLÉ
WITH ESPRESSO CARAMEL SAUCE

Chocolate is the king of all soufflés. Since they must be made at the last minute, I use the final soufflé preparation time as a period when guests get to stretch their legs and prepare themselves for the grand finale. It is also a good time to get someone else started doing the dishes!

SERVES 6

Chocolate Soufflé

3 large egg yolks

⅓ cup granulated sugar

½ cup all-purpose flour

⅛ teaspoon salt

1½ cups milk

4 ounces bittersweet chocolate, finely chopped

1¼ cups (about 10 large) egg whites

½ teaspoon cream of tartar

Pinch of salt

2½ cups Espresso Caramel Sauce (page 229)

Equipment

A 2-quart round ovenproof dish, buttered and sugared

In a stainless steel bowl, whisk together the egg yolks and the sugar. Whisk in the flour and salt.

In a small heavy-bottomed saucepan bring the milk to a full boil over medium-high heat. Pour the milk into the egg mixture all at once and whisk the mixture until smooth and thick. Add the chopped chocolate and whisk until smooth.

Transfer the chocolate soufflé base to a clean bowl, covering the surface directly with plastic wrap. Refrigerate until cold.

Preheat the oven to 350 degrees.

In the bowl of an electric mixer, whip the egg whites on high speed until frothy. Add the cream of tartar and salt and continue whipping until the egg whites are stiff yet still shiny and moist.

Fold the egg whites into the chocolate mixture in two additions. Work gently but quickly to incorporate them.

Carefully place the batter in the prepared dish. Gently tap the soufflé dish on the counter to remove any air bubbles. Bake until the soufflé is a nice brown color on top and feels set when gently touched on top and sides, 35 to 40 minutes. Present the soufflé at the table. Serve immediately with the espresso caramel sauce.

AHEAD-OF-TIME NOTES

The soufflé base can be made a day in advance.
The egg whites must be whipped and the soufflé baked just before serving.

CHOCOLATE PEPPERMINT BROWNIES

This is a recipe adapted from my grandmother, after whom I am named. She made cookies from this recipe;
I prefer baking it in one pan because it is moister. Use either loose tea leaves or tea from tea bags.

24 BROWNIES

Brownies

12 ounces unsweetened chocolate,
  finely chopped

12 ounces (3 sticks) unsalted butter, softened

1 tablespoon peppermint tea

3 cups granulated sugar

6 large eggs

1½ cups all-purpose flour

Pinch of salt

Glaze

6 ounces bittersweet chocolate, finely chopped

3 tablespoons unsalted butter

Equipment

A 9- by 13-inch baking pan,
  buttered and floured

BROWNIES

Preheat the oven to 350 degrees.

In a double boiler over hot water, melt the chocolate and the butter, making sure that the water does not touch the bottom of the pan holding the chocolate. Whisk until smooth.

In a food processor, finely grind the peppermint tea with the sugar.

In a medium mixing bowl, whisk together the eggs and the peppermint sugar until well combined. Stir in the melted chocolate mixture. Stir in the flour and salt. Spread the batter into the prepared pan. Bake until a skewer inserted in the middle comes out almost completely clean, 30 to 35 minutes. Do not overcook.

Let the brownies cool to room temperature.

GLAZE

Melt the chocolate and the butter in a double boiler over hot water, making sure that the water does not touch the bottom of the pan holding the chocolate. Whisk until smooth. Pour the glaze over the brownies.

Let the glaze set and then cut the brownies.

AHEAD-OF-TIME NOTES

Like all brownies, these are best eaten the day they are baked. Store in an airtight container at room temperature.

GATEAU ROYALE

This recipe was given to me by my first cooking instructor and mentor, Lois Murphy. After 15 years it is still one of my favorite recipes. Serve with Cappuccino Ice Cream (page 241) and Butterscotch Sauce (page 231).

SERVES 8 TO 10

8 ounces bittersweet chocolate, finely chopped

½ pound (2 sticks) unsalted butter, softened

1¼ cups granulated sugar

4 large eggs

5 tablespoons cornstarch

2 tablespoons Grand Marnier

Equipment

A 9-inch round by 3-inch high cake pan,
   the bottom lined with parchment paper

A baking pan large enough to hold the
   cake pan

Melt the chocolate in a double boiler over hot water, making sure that the water does not touch the bottom of the pan holding the chocolate. Whisk until smooth. Cool to room temperature. Add the butter to the chocolate and whisk until smooth.

Preheat the oven to 350 degrees.

In the bowl of an electric mixer combine the sugar and the eggs. Using the whisk attachment on high speed, whip the egg mixture until thick. Reduce to medium-low speed and add the chocolate butter mixture. Stir in the cornstarch and then the Grand Marnier. Spread the batter into the prepared cake pan. If you are using a two-piece pan, wrap the bottom and sides in foil.

Place the cake pan in the baking pan. Place the baking pan on a rack in the middle of the oven. Fill the baking pan with water so that the water comes about a third up the sides of the pan. Bake until the cake is crusty on top and a skewer inserted in the middle still has a wet crumb, 45 to 50 minutes.

Remove the cake pan from the baking pan. Cool the cake on a rack for several hours. Unmold the cake by turning it upside down on a flat plate. Remove the parchment paper and invert the cake again right side up. Dust with powdered sugar or cocoa powder before serving.

AHEAD-OF-TIME NOTES

The cake can be made a day in advance. Store at room temperature.

CHOCOLATE-FILLED FILO TRIANGLES

Michael, the photographer for this book, likes to serve these with vanilla ice cream!

SERVES 8

6 ounces bittersweet chocolate

½ cup granulated sugar

8 sheets filo, defrosted

8 tablespoons (1 stick) unsalted butter, melted

Equipment

An 11- by 17-inch baking tray, lined with parchment paper

Break up 4 ounces of chocolate into ½-ounce pieces. Set aside.

In a food processor, finely grind the remaining chocolate with the sugar.

Lay 8 sheets of filo out on top of each other.

Place one sheet lengthwise on the work surface. Keep the remaining sheets covered with a damp towel.

Brush the sheet with some melted butter. Sprinkle with 1½ tablespoons of the sugar mixture. Place a second sheet over the sugared sheet. Butter the second sheet and sprinkle with the sugar mixture. Add 2 more sheets, buttering and sprinkling between each.

Cut the filo horizontally into 4 even strips. Starting at the left side of one of the strips, place a ½-ounce piece of chocolate 2 inches from the end. Fold the filo that is to the left of the piece of chocolate over the chocolate toward the back side of the strip, making a 3-inch triangle. The left end of the filo should be even with the back edge. Fold the piece of chocolate to the right, over itself, retaining the triangular shape. Fold the chocolate piece toward the front edge of the strip. Continue wrapping the chocolate, alternating the direction with each fold, until you get to the end. (It is like folding a flag.) Wrap the other strips in the same manner.

With the remaining sheets, make 4 more chocolate-filled triangles.

Preheat the oven to 350 degrees. Place the triangles on the baking sheet. Bake until golden brown, about 10 minutes. Serve warm.

AHEAD-OF-TIME NOTES

The triangles are best served the day they are made. They can be reheated.

CHOCOLATE BANANA FANTASY

My brothers love to have me make them chocolate-covered bananas. Here I combine the bananas with another chocolate and banana combination.

SERVES 6

Banana Sherbet

4 very ripe bananas

4 cups buttermilk

½ cup granulated sugar

¾ cup light corn syrup

¾ cup dark corn syrup

¼ teaspoon salt

6 tablespoons rum

Chocolate Sabayon

1 tablespoon cocoa powder

⅓ cup granulated sugar

Pinch of salt

½ cup water

2 tablespoons rum

6 large egg yolks

3 ounces bittersweet chocolate, finely chopped

¾ cup heavy whipping cream

BANANA SHERBET

In a food processor purée the bananas until smooth.

In a medium mixing bowl combine the banana purée, buttermilk, sugar, light and dark corn syrups, salt, and rum. Stir until combined.

According to manufacturer's instructions, freeze in an ice cream machine.

CHOCOLATE SABAYON

Fill a medium mixing bowl ⅓ full of ice water. Set aside.

Fill a medium saucepan ⅓ full of water. Bring the water to a low boil.

In a medium mixing bowl, combine the cocoa powder, sugar, salt, water, rum, and egg yolks. Whisk until well blended. Set the bowl into the saucepan of boiling water. Again, make sure that the bowl fits snugly in the saucepan; at the same time, the bottom of the bowl should not touch the water. The bowl mustn't be too deep nor the water level too high. Cook the cocoa mixture, whisking constantly, until thick, about 3 minutes.

Remove the bowl from the heat and whisk in the chopped chocolate. Place the bowl of sabayon in the bowl of ice water. Cool the sabayon to room temperature, whisking occasionally.

In a medium mixing bowl, whip the cream until soft peaks form. Fold the cream into the cooled sabayon. Refrigerate the sabayon until you are ready to serve the dessert.

Chocolate-covered Bananas

7 ounces bittersweet chocolate, finely chopped
3 bananas

CHOCOLATE-COVERED BANANAS

Put the chocolate in a medium stainless steel mixing bowl. Set the bowl into the saucepan of boiling water. Make sure the bowl fits snugly in the saucepan; at the same time, the bottom of the bowl should not touch the water. The bowl mustn't be too deep or the water level too high. Melt the chocolate. Stir until smooth. Set aside.

Slice the bananas in half lengthwise and then into thirds.

With a fork, dip the banana pieces into the melted chocolate. Place them on a wire mesh rack and freeze 1 to 2 hours.

ASSEMBLY

Put some of the banana sherbet on each of 6 plates or in a large bowl with low sides. Dollop some of the chocolate sabayon over the sherbet. Place several chocolate-covered banana slices around the sherbet. Serve at once.

AHEAD-OF-TIME NOTES

The sherbet, sabayon, and chocolate-covered bananas can all be made a day in advance.

SUMMER BERRIES

♦♦♦

*Strawberries, raspberries, blueberries, blackberries,
olallieberries, marionberries (both from the blackberry family), golden
raspberries, black raspberries. Berries with a little sabayon
are a dessert by themselves. Make berries one
of several elements in a dessert and the dessert is lifted to a
whole new level of taste and complexity. However you
put berries in a dessert, do not disguise their inherent flavors. In almost
all these recipes the berries are interchangeable. If you find
an abundance of strawberries in your garden, substitute them for the
raspberries in the champagne cream cake, or if the olallieberries
at the market simply can't be resisted, use them in the cream cheese soufflés.*

Warm Zabaglione with Strawberries 57

Strawberry Gratin 58

White Chocolate Mousse with Raspberries and White Chocolate Brittle 59

Oat Crisps with Blueberries and Crème Fraîche 61

Caramel Bavarian with Berries 62

Souffléed Crêpe with Mixed Berries 63

Raspberry Cream Cheese Soufflés 64

Blueberry Lemon Cheesecake with a Cornmeal Crust 65

Raspberry Spritzer 66

Blueberry Pie 68

Caramel Almond Tartlets with Warm Blueberries 69

Mixed Berry Buns 71

Strawberry Crostata 72

Raspberry Champagne Cream Cake 73

Strawberry Grand Marnier Trifle 74

Strawberry Madeira Napoleon 76

Raspberry Tartlets with Ginger Pastry Cream 77

Raspberry Lemon Buttermilk Pie 78

Honey Blueberry Cake 79

Blackberry Chiffon Roll 81

Goat Cheese Cake with Mixed Berries 83

WARM ZABAGLIONE WITH STRAWBERRIES

*Warm zabaglione was very popular in the fifties and sixties. It's been "out" for so long that
it's time to bring it back. It's delicious, quick to make, and a light dessert for those watching their waistlines.
Serve with the Macadamia Nut Biscotti on page 204.*

SERVES 8

10 cups quartered, hulled strawberries

6 large egg yolks

¾ cup granulated sugar

7 tablespoons good quality marsala

Pinch of salt

Place the strawberries in 8 bowls or wide wine glasses. Set aside.

Fill a medium saucepan ⅓ full of water. Bring the water to a low boil.

In a medium stainless steel bowl, lightly whisk together the egg yolks and sugar. Add the marsala and the pinch of salt.

Set the bowl into the saucepan of boiling water. Make sure the bowl fits snugly in the saucepan; at the same time, the bottom of the bowl should not touch the water. The bowl mustn't be too deep nor the water level too high. Whisk the marsala mixture vigorously and constantly until thick, 2 to 3 minutes.

Remove the bowl from the heat, spoon the zabaglione over the strawberries, and serve at once.

AHEAD-OF-TIME NOTES

Warm zabaglione must be served immediately; it can't be made in advance.

STRAWBERRY GRATIN

I use this recipe when I need a very easy-to-prepare yet wonderful dessert.
Serve the gratin at the table, impressing everyone with its beautiful appearance! You can substitute
practically any type of summer berries or fruits.

SERVES 6

8 cups quartered strawberries

1½ cups sour cream

Pinch of salt

2 tablespoons half-and-half

½ cup firmly packed dark brown sugar

Equipment

A 9½- by 13-inch ovenproof baking dish

Preheat the broiler.

Place the strawberries in the bottom of the baking dish.

In a mixing bowl, whisk together the sour cream, salt, and half-and-half. Spoon the mixture evenly over the strawberries.

Sprinkle the brown sugar on top of the sour cream mixture. Place the dish under the broiler and broil until the brown sugar has melted. Serve immediately.

AHEAD-OF-TIME NOTES

The strawberry gratin cannot be made in advance, but it is so simple that you won't need to.

WHITE CHOCOLATE MOUSSE WITH RASPBERRIES AND WHITE CHOCOLATE BRITTLE

I prefer white chocolate to dark chocolate when served with raspberries. White chocolate has a softer flavor and will not overpower or be too harsh for the raspberries' delicate perfume.

SERVES 8

7 large egg yolks

½ cup granulated sugar

⅓ cup brandy

⅓ cup water

1 tablespoon freshly squeezed lemon juice

5 ounces white chocolate, very finely chopped

1½ cups heavy whipping cream

10 cups ripe raspberries

A 10- by 10-inch piece White Chocolate Raspberry Brittle (page 191)

Fill a medium saucepan ⅓ full of water. Bring the water to a simmer.

Fill a medium bowl ⅓ full of ice water. Set aside.

In a medium mixing bowl, whisk together the egg yolks and the sugar. Add the brandy, water, and lemon juice. Set the bowl into the saucepan of boiling water. Make sure the bowl fits snugly in the saucepan; at the same time, the bottom of the bowl should not touch the water. The bowl mustn't be too deep nor the water level too high. Whisk the mixture vigorously and constantly until thick, 2 or 3 minutes.

Remove the bowl from the heat and whisk in the white chocolate until smooth.

Place the bowl of the white chocolate mixture in the bowl of ice water and whisk until it reaches room temperature.

In a medium mixing bowl, whip the cream to soft peaks. Fold the cream into the cooled white chocolate mixture. Refrigerate the mousse until you are ready to serve it.

FINISHING THE DESSERT

Place about a cup of raspberries in each of 8 bowls and spoon some of the white chocolate mousse on the top. Garnish the mousse with the white chocolate raspberry brittle. Serve immediately.

AHEAD-OF-TIME NOTES

The mousse is best eaten the day it is made.

OAT CRISPS WITH BLUEBERRIES AND CRÈME FRAÎCHE

This dessert could be served for breakfast as well. For a more elaborate presentation you can stack the oat crisps alternately with the berries and the crème fraîche.

SERVES 6

2½ tablespoons unsalted butter, melted

¼ cup firmly packed dark brown sugar

2 tablespoons granulated sugar

2 tablespoons dark corn syrup

1 cup rolled oats (not instant)

2 pints fresh blueberries

1 cup crème fraîche

Preheat the oven to 350 degrees.

In a medium bowl combine the melted butter, brown sugar, granulated sugar, and the corn syrup. Stir in the oats and mix well.

Place 1 tablespoon of the oat mixture for each crisp onto on a parchment-lined baking tray. Fill the tray with tablespoons of oat mixture, leaving several inches between each—they spread as they bake. Bake the crisps until golden brown and bubbly, about 15 minutes. Let them cool for several minutes before removing them from the baking tray.

For each person, serve 2 oat crisps with some blueberries and crème fraîche.

AHEAD-OF-TIME NOTES

The oat crisps can be made a day in advance. Store at room temperature in an airtight container.

CARAMEL BAVARIAN WITH BERRIES

This Caramel Bavarian is so smooth you don't even need a sauce.

SERVES 8

½ cup freshly squeezed orange juice

1½ teaspoons powdered gelatin

6 large egg yolks

2 teaspoons cornstarch

1 cup granulated sugar

½ cup water

1½ cups milk

1 cup heavy whipping cream

1 pint raspberries

1 pint blackberries

Equipment

A 9½- by 4-inch terrine mold, lined with plastic wrap

In a small saucepan, mix together the orange juice and the gelatin. Let sit for 10 minutes.

In a medium stainless steel mixing bowl, whisk together the egg yolks and the cornstarch. Set aside.

In a medium saucepan, stir together the sugar and the water. Cook over medium heat until the sugar dissolves. Increase to high heat and cook the sugar until it is golden colored. (Do not stir after you increase the heat.) Remove the pan from the heat and carefully stir in a few tablespoons of milk. Let the caramel bubble and subside. Add a few more tablespoons of milk. Slowly add the remaining milk.

Fill a medium bowl ⅓ full of ice water. Set aside.

Fill a medium saucepan ⅓ full of water. Bring the water to a low boil.

Whisk the milk into the egg yolks. Set the bowl into the saucepan of boiling water, making sure that the water doesn't touch the bottom of the bowl. Cook the caramel mixture, stirring continually, until it thickens slightly and coats the back of a spoon, 3 to 5 minutes. Remove the bowl from the heat.

Dissolve the gelatin over low heat and stir it into the caramel mixture. Place the bowl into the bowl of ice water. Stirring constantly, let the mixture thicken. If it gets lumpy, whisk until smooth.

Whip the cream to soft peaks and fold in the caramel mixture. Pour into the mold. Chill until set.

Unmold the cream onto a large plate. Present the cream with the raspberries and blackberries.

AHEAD-OF-TIME NOTES

The Bavarian can be made a day in advance. Unmold and garnish with berries just before serving.

SOUFFLÉED CRÊPE WITH MIXED BERRIES

Light and airy, this dessert is mostly fruit with just a little bit of sweetness lest you feel deprived. Good for the dieters.

SERVES 6 TO 8

2 large eggs

½ cup all-purpose flour

½ cup milk

1 tablespoon granulated sugar

1½ teaspoons finely chopped orange zest

1 tablespoon unsalted butter, softened

1 pint each of blueberries, strawberries, and blackberries

1 cup sweetened Raspberry Purée (page 238)

Equipment

A 9-inch sauté pan

Preheat the oven to 375 degrees.

In a medium mixing bowl, lightly whisk together the eggs. Sift the flour into the eggs and stir until combined. Mix in the milk, sugar, and orange zest.

Heat the empty sauté pan in the oven for about 5 minutes. Remove from the oven and add the butter, spreading it evenly over the bottom of the pan. When the butter has melted, pour the batter into the pan and bake until golden brown and puffy, 20 to 25 minutes. Remove the crêpe from the pan with a large spatula.

Serve the souffléed crêpe immediately with a bowl of the fresh berries and a pitcher of the raspberry purée on the side, or place the berries in the middle of the crêpe and serve immediately.

AHEAD-OF-TIME NOTES

The crêpe batter can be made a couple of hours in advance.

RASPBERRY CREAM CHEESE SOUFFLÉS

These little soufflés aren't true soufflés in the sense that they don't puff up dramatically, but they do have the light texture that good soufflés should have. Unlike real soufflés, they can be reheated, making it easier on the cook.

SERVES 6

2 cups raspberries

1 tablespoon all-purpose flour

1 cup granulated sugar

8 ounces cream cheese

2 large egg yolks

1 teaspoon finely chopped lemon zest

2 tablespoons freshly squeezed lemon juice

4 large egg whites

Powdered sugar for dusting the tops
   of the soufflés

Equipment

Six 10-ounce ovenproof dishes,
   buttered and sugared

Preheat the oven to 350 degrees.

In a small bowl, combine the raspberries and the flour. Divide the raspberries among the individual ramekins. Set aside.

Place ¾ cup of the sugar and the cream cheese in the bowl of an electric mixer. Using the paddle attachment on medium speed mix well. Add the egg yolks, chopped lemon zest, and lemon juice. Mix the ingredients until smooth.

In a clean bowl of an electric mixer using the whip attachment on high speed, whip the egg whites until frothy. Add the remaining ¼ cup sugar in a steady stream and continue to whip until soft peaks form. Fold the egg whites into the cream cheese mixture. Gently pour the soufflé mixture into the prepared ramekins. Bake the soufflés for about 20 minutes until golden brown on top and a knife inserted in the center comes out almost completely clean. The very center should still be creamy. Invert the soufflés onto plates, raspberry side up, and serve immediately.

AHEAD-OF-TIME NOTES

The raspberry cream cheese soufflés can be made an hour or so in advance and reheated for 5 minutes.

BLUEBERRY LEMON CHEESECAKE
WITH A CORNMEAL CRUST

Serving the blueberries on top of the cheesecake instead of baking them inside keeps the blueberry flavor fresh.

SERVES 8 TO 10

Cornmeal Crust

8 tablespoons (1 stick) unsalted butter, softened

¼ cup granulated sugar

½ cup all-purpose flour

½ cup yellow cornmeal

Pinch of salt

Lemon Cheesecake

2 pounds cream cheese, softened

1 cup mascarpone, softened

1½ cups granulated sugar

2 large eggs

2 teaspoons finely chopped lemon zest

3 tablespoons freshly squeezed lemon juice

Blueberry Topping

3 cups fresh blueberries

½ cup granulated sugar

1 tablespoon water

2 teaspoons freshly squeezed lemon juice

Equipment

A 9-inch springform pan, the bottom and sides wrapped in aluminum foil

A rectangular baking pan large enough to hold the springform pan

CORNMEAL CRUST

Preheat the oven to 350 degrees.

In the bowl of an electric mixer, combine the butter and sugar. Using the paddle on medium speed, mix until smooth. On low speed, mix in the flour, cornmeal, and salt until crumbly. Press into the bottom of the springform pan. Bake until light brown, about 20 minutes. Set aside.

LEMON CHEESECAKE

Decrease the oven temperature to 325 degrees.

In a bowl of an electric mixer combine the cream cheese, mascarpone, and sugar. Using the paddle attachment on medium speed, mix until smooth. Mix in the eggs, lemon zest, and lemon juice.

Spread the batter over the crust. Place the springform pan in the rectangular baking pan. Fill the baking pan ⅓ full of hot water. Bake in the waterbath until all but the very center is set, about 1 hour.

Remove the cheesecake from the waterbath. With a knife, loosen the edges of the cheesecake from the pan. (This will prevent cracks in the middle.) Refrigerate until cold.

BLUEBERRY TOPPING

In a saucepan combine the blueberries, sugar, water, and lemon juice. Over medium-low heat, cook the mixture 5–10 minutes until thick. Cool to room temperature. Spread over the cheesecake.

AHEAD-OF-TIME NOTES

The cheesecake will keep 1 to 2 days in the refrigerator. Place the topping on the cheesecake just before serving.

RASPBERRY SPRITZER

The perfect refresher for a hot summer afternoon. All that's missing is the lounge chair by the pool.

1⅔ cups unsweetened Raspberry Purée
   (page 238)

1 cup granulated sugar

¼ cup freshly squeezed lemon juice

Pinch of salt

8 cups seltzer

6 scoops Vanilla Ice Cream (page 240)

Equipment

6 tall clear glasses

In a small pitcher, combine the raspberry purée, sugar, lemon juice, and salt. Mix until the sugar is dissolved.

Spoon about ¼ cup of the raspberry mixture into each glass. Pour 1 cup of the seltzer into each glass. Mix well. Place a scoop of ice cream in each glass. Serve immediately.

AHEAD-OF-TIME NOTES

The ingredients can all be assembled in advance, but do not combine them until the last moment.

BLUEBERRY PIE

Imagine sitting on a porch in the middle of summer lazily enjoying a piece of blueberry pie as the rest of the world (and everyone in it) rushes madly about.

SERVES 8

½ cup all-purpose flour

1 cup plus 1 teaspoon granulated sugar

Large pinch ground mace

¼ teaspoon salt

1 teaspoon finely chopped lemon zest

2½ pints fresh blueberries

One 9-inch uncooked pie shell with a flat edge (page 226)

1 unbaked pie top (page 226)

2 tablespoons heavy whipping cream

Preheat the oven to 375 degrees.

In a medium bowl combine the flour, 1 cup sugar, mace, salt, and lemon zest. Stir in the blueberries. Place the blueberry mixture in the unbaked pie shell.

Lay the pie top over the blueberries. Fold the edge of the top crust under the edge of the bottom crust. Press the two doughs together to make sure that the pie is sealed. With a fork, press a decorative pattern into the pie edge. Cut four 1-inch slits in the middle of the top of the pie. Brush the pie with the cream. Sprinkle the remaining teaspoon of sugar over the top.

Bake the pie until it starts to brown, about 40 minutes. Decrease the oven temperature to 350 degrees and continue to bake the pie until it is golden brown and the blueberry mixture is thick and bubbly, 45 minutes to 1 hour more.

AHEAD-OF-TIME NOTES

The pie is best eaten the day it is baked. Serve warm or at room temperature. Store at room temperature.

CARAMEL ALMOND TARTLETS WITH WARM BLUEBERRIES

This dessert combines my husband's three favorite dessert flavors—caramel, almonds, and berries. It can also be made into one 9-inch tart. These tartlets are equally good served warm or at room temperature.

SERVES 6

Almond Tartlets

2 cups (8 ounces) whole natural almonds, toasted

6 prebaked four-inch tartlet shells (page 226)

1½ cups granulated sugar

⅓ cup water

1 cup plus 2 tablespoons heavy whipping cream

1 large egg, lightly beaten

Warm Blueberries

2½ cups blueberries

¼ cup granulated sugar

3 cups Whipped Cream (page 225)

ALMOND TARTLETS

Preheat the oven to 325 degrees.

Coarsely chop the almonds. Scatter them in the bottoms of the tart shells.

In a small heavy-bottomed saucepan, combine the sugar and water. Cook over medium heat until the sugar dissolves. Increase to high heat and continue to cook until the sugar caramelizes and is a golden amber color. (Do not stir once you increase the heat.) Remove the saucepan from the heat and let the bubbles subside for a couple of seconds. Carefully stir in 2 tablespoons of the cream. The caramel will sputter as you add the cream, so stir carefully and make sure that the bubbles subside before slowly adding the rest of the cream. Cool for 5 minutes. Whisk in the beaten egg. Pour the caramel cream into the tartlet shells over the almonds. Bake the tartlets until thick and bubbly, 15 to 20 minutes.

WARM BLUEBERRIES

In a large sauté pan, combine the sugar and the blueberries. Cook over medium-high heat until the berries burst and start to give off some of their juice, 2 to 3 minutes.

Place an almond tartlet on each of six plates. Top with whipped cream and some blueberries.

AHEAD-OF-TIME NOTES

The tartlets are best served the day they are made. They can be reheated. Store at room temperature. Prepare the berries just before serving.

MIXED BERRY BUNS

Like brioche but loaded with berries, these little buns guarantee a wonderful start to any day.
Bake these in the morning to get everyone out of bed!

SERVES 8

Buns

2¼ cups all-purpose flour

6 tablespoons granulated sugar

½ teaspoon salt

1 teaspoon ground ginger

¼ teaspoon ground white pepper

1 tablespoon dry yeast

¼ cup warm water

3 large eggs

12 tablespoons (1½ sticks) unsalted butter, softened

Berry Filling

½ pint raspberries

½ pint blackberries

½ cup dark brown sugar

1 tablespoon cornstarch

Equipment

A 10-inch round pan, buttered

BUNS

Sift together the flour, sugar, salt, ginger, and white pepper. Set aside.

In a small mixing bowl whisk together the yeast and the warm water. Let rest for 10 minutes. Add the eggs and mix until combined.

Place the dry ingredients in the bowl of an electric mixer. Using the paddle attachment on low speed, pour in the egg mixture and mix until combined. Add the butter. Increase to medium speed and mix until the butter is completely incorporated and the dough is smooth.

Place the dough in a buttered bowl and cover with a towel. Let rise until doubled, about 2 hours.

Place the dough on a lightly floured work surface. Punch it down with your hands and divide it into 8 pieces. Roll each piece into a ball. Arrange in the pan.

BERRY FILLING

In a medium bowl gently combine the raspberries, blackberries, brown sugar, and cornstarch.

With your finger, make a 1-inch hole in the center of each bun. Place some of the berry mixture in each hole. Cover the buns with a towel and let rise until doubled. (Alternatively, the filled buns can proof overnight in the refrigerator. Let them sit for 15 minutes at room temperature before baking.)

Preheat the oven to 350 degrees.

Bake until golden brown, 35 to 45 minutes.

AHEAD-OF-TIME NOTES

The buns are best the day they are baked.

STRAWBERRY CROSTATA

Crostata means pie or tart in Italian. I added the jam for a more intense strawberry flavor.

2 cups plus 1 tablespoon all-purpose flour

⅔ cup plus 1 tablespoon granulated sugar

8 tablespoons (1 stick) cold unsalted butter

2 large eggs

1 large egg yolk

½ cup strawberry jam

1 pint strawberries, hulled and cut in half

In a medium bowl, combine 2 cups of the flour, ⅔ cup of the granulated sugar and the butter. Mix the ingredients with a pastry blender until the mixture has the texture of cornmeal. Add 1 egg and the egg yolk and mix until the dough comes together, 1 to 2 minutes. Divide the dough into 2 pieces. Chill both pieces until firm, about 30 minutes.

On a lightly floured work surface, roll one of the pieces of dough into a 10-inch circle. Place the circle on a baking sheet. Roll the second piece ¼ inch thick and cut it into ½-inch strips. Refrigerate both the dough circle and the strips until firm, at least 30 minutes.

Preheat the oven to 375 degrees.

Spread the jam over the 10-inch round piece of dough, leaving a 1-inch edge all around. In a medium bowl gently combine the strawberries with the remaining 1 tablespoon each of sugar and flour. Place the berries on top of the jam.

Lightly beat the remaining egg and brush it on the 1-inch edge of the dough circle. Lay the strips of dough on top of the strawberries, letting each strip end on the egg-washed part of the circle. Fold the edges of the dough circle ¼ inch over the ends of the lattice. Brush the edges and lattice with more of the beaten egg. Bake the crostata until golden brown, 30 to 35 minutes.

AHEAD-OF-TIME NOTES

The crostata dough can be made and rolled a day in advance and refrigerated. The crostata should be assembled and eaten the day it is baked.

RASPBERRY CHAMPAGNE CREAM CAKE

This is my favorite nonchocolate cake to make for birthdays.

SERVES 8 TO 10

Cake

6 egg yolks

⅔ cup champagne

⅓ cup granulated sugar

¾ cup heavy whipping cream

2 recipes Vanilla Genoise (page 237)

⅔ cup sweetened Raspberry Purée
(page 238)

Frosting

1¼ cups heavy whipping cream

2 tablespoons granulated sugar

½ teaspoon vanilla extract

½ pint raspberries

Equipment

A 9-inch round by 3-inch high
springform pan, the bottom lined with
parchment paper

CAKE

Fill a medium mixing bowl ⅓ full of ice water.

Fill a medium saucepan ⅓ full of water and bring it to a boil.

In a medium mixing bowl, combine the egg yolks, champagne, and sugar. Whisk until well blended. Set the bowl into the saucepan of water, making sure the water doesn't touch the bottom of the bowl. Cook the mixture, stirring constantly, until thick, about 3 minutes. Place the bowl in the bowl of ice water. Cool, whisking occasionally.

In a medium mixing bowl, whip cream until soft peaks form. Fold the cream into the cooled sabayon.

With a serrated knife, cut the vanilla genoise into three 9-inch circles. Cut each circle in half horizontally, making 6 circles altogether.

Place a cake circle in the bottom of the cake pan. Spread 2 tablespoons of the raspberry purée evenly over the cake. Spread about ¼ cup of the champagne sabayon on top. Continue this layering process, ending with a layer of raspberry purée.

FROSTING

Chill the cake for at least 1 hour. Invert the cake and remove the cake pan and the parchment paper. In a medium mixing bowl, whip the cream with the sugar and vanilla extract until stiff. Frost the sides and top of the cake with the whipped cream. Decorate the top of the cake with the raspberries. Refrigerate the cake until you are ready to serve it.

AHEAD-OF-TIME NOTES

The raspberry cream cake can be assembled a day in advance. Frost the cake the day you serve it.

STRAWBERRY GRAND MARNIER TRIFLE

Here I have made the trifle in a baking pan so that the pieces look more finished and not quite so rustic.

8 large egg yolks
½ cup plus 2 tablespoons granulated sugar
Pinch of salt
¼ cup Grand Marnier
½ cup freshly squeezed orange juice
1 cup heavy whipping cream
3 pints strawberries, hulled
1 recipe Vanilla Genoise (page 237)

Equipment
A 9- by 13-inch baking pan

Fill a large bowl ⅓ full of ice water. Set aside.

Fill a medium saucepan ⅓ full of water and bring it to a boil.

In a medium stainless steel mixing bowl, whisk together the egg yolks, ½ cup of the sugar, and the salt. Whisk in the Grand Marnier and the orange juice. Set the bowl into the saucepan of boiling water, making sure that the water doesn't touch the bottom of the bowl. Whisk the mixture constantly until thick, 2 to 3 minutes. Place the bowl in the bowl of ice water and whisk until it is cool.

In a medium mixing bowl, whip the cream until thick. Fold the cream into the cooled Grand Marnier mixture. Refrigerate.

In a food processor, coarsely chop the strawberries with the remaining 2 tablespoons of sugar, using on-off turns.

Using a serrated knife, cut the cake into 4 even rectangles. Slice each piece in half horizontally, making 8 pieces altogether.

Place a layer of strawberries in the bottom of the baking pan. Top with a little more than a cup of the Grand Marnier sabayon. Cover the sabayon with a layer of genoise. The cake does not have to be in one piece; it can be pieced together. Repeat this layering process, ending with a layer of sabayon. There should be three layers of cake. Refrigerate the trifle for at least 6 hours before serving. To serve, cut the trifle with a sharp knife.

AHEAD-OF-TIME NOTES

The trifle can be made up to two days in advance. Store covered in plastic wrap in the refrigerator.

STRAWBERRY MADEIRA NAPOLEON

This napoleon is layered with sour cream rather than the traditional pastry cream. The result is a clean cool taste.

SERVES 6

1 pound Puff Pastry (page 234)

2 pints strawberries

6 tablespoons plus 2 teaspoons granulated sugar

2 tablespoons Madeira

¾ cup sour cream

½ teaspoon vanilla extract

confectioners' sugar

PUFF PASTRY

Divide the puff pastry in two. Put one piece in the refrigerator. Roll the remaining piece into a 12- by 9-inch rectangle. Be sure to keep the top and bottom of the pastry lightly floured so it does not stick to the table or the rolling pin. Keep the puff pastry in an even shape as you roll. With a fork, punch small holes all over the pastry. With a sharp knife, cut the puff pastry into 3- x 4-inch rectangles. Roll out the other half of puff pastry in the same manner. There should be 18 rectangles. Freeze for at least 1 hour.

Preheat the oven to 375 degrees.

Place the frozen puff pastry in single layers on baking sheets. Place an inverted wire mesh rack or another baking sheet on top of the puff pastry. (This will prevent the pastry from rising as it cooks.) Bake until golden, 10 to 15 minutes.

FINISHING

Cut the strawberries in half. In a mixing bowl gently stir together the strawberries, 6 tablespoons of the sugar, and the Madeira. Marinate for 10 minutes.

In a small bowl stir together the sour cream, the remaining 2 teaspoons of sugar, and vanilla.

Place a piece of puff pastry on each plate. Spread 1 tablespoon of the sour cream on top. Spoon some strawberries and a little of their juice over the sour cream. Add a second piece of puff pastry and layer in the same manner. Top with a third piece of puff pastry. Dust with confectioners' sugar. Serve at once.

AHEAD-OF-TIME NOTES

The strawberries should be prepared at the last minute. The sour cream mixture can be made a day in advance.

RASPBERRY TARTLETS
WITH GINGER PASTRY CREAM

A simple, fresh-looking raspberry tartlet perked up with the addition of a light ginger pastry cream.
This can be made in a large tart but it is not as pretty when cut.

SERVES 6

6 large egg yolks

⅓ cup granulated sugar

Pinch of salt

2 tablespoons cornstarch

1⅔ cups milk

1 ounce (3-inch piece) fresh ginger,
   cut into 4 pieces

½ cup heavy whipping cream

6 prebaked 4-inch tartlet shells (page 226)

2 pints raspberries

In a medium mixing bowl combine the egg yolks, sugar, and salt in a mixing bowl and whisk until well blended. Stir in the cornstarch.

In a heavy-bottomed saucepan combine the milk and the ginger. Scald the milk over medium high heat. Cover the saucepan and remove it from the heat. Let the ginger infuse in the milk for 15 minutes. Uncover the saucepan and again scald the milk. Whisk it slowly into the egg-sugar mixture.

Transfer the ginger milk back into the saucepan. Cook it over medium-low heat, stirring constantly until thick, making sure to scrape the bottom of the saucepan, about 5 minutes. Strain the pastry cream through a medium sieve into a bowl. Place plastic wrap directly onto the surface of the pastry cream to prevent a skin from forming. Refrigerate until cold.

In a medium mixing bowl, whip the cream until soft peaks form. Fold the ginger pastry cream into the cream. Refrigerate until you are ready to serve.

Spoon some of the ginger pastry cream into the bottom of each tart shell. Arrange the raspberries on top of the ginger cream in a circular pattern. Serve immediately.

AHEAD-OF-TIME NOTES

The ginger pastry cream can be made a couple of days in advance, but do not beat or fold in the whipped cream until the day you are going to serve the tartlets. The tartlet shells can be made several days in advance and frozen. Bake them the day you plan to serve them.

RASPBERRY LEMON BUTTERMILK PIE

My sister-in-law is a lemon lover. I am always trying to think up new lemon desserts for her.
This is one of her favorites. You can subsititute blueberries or blackberries.

SERVES 6 TO 8

1½ cups granulated sugar

3 large eggs

1½ cups buttermilk

2 tablespoons heavy whipping cream

1 tablespoon freshly squeezed lemon juice

¼ teaspoon vanilla extract

8 tablespoons (1 stick) unsalted butter, melted

2 teaspoons finely chopped lemon zest

⅓ cup all-purpose flour

¼ teaspoon salt

Pinch of ground nutmeg

½ pint raspberries

A 9-inch prebaked pie shell (page 226)

Preheat the oven to 325 degrees.

In a medium mixing bowl whisk together the sugar and eggs. Add the buttermilk, cream, lemon juice, vanilla extract, and butter. Whisk until smooth. Stir in the lemon zest, flour, salt, and nutmeg.

Place the raspberries in the bottom of the prebaked pie shell. Pour the buttermilk mixture over the raspberries. Bake the pie until set, about 50 minutes. Let cool to room temperature before serving.

AHEAD-OF-TIME NOTES

The pie is best eaten the day it is baked.

HONEY BLUEBERRY CAKE

*This is a pretty cake. The honey in the cake and the honey glaze give it a golden brown color,
with flecks of blue from the berries. Serve with Orange Honey Ice Cream (page 242).*

A 9-INCH BUNDT CAKE

½ pound (2 sticks) unsalted butter, softened

¼ cup granulated sugar

1¼ cups honey

4 large eggs, slightly beaten

2 tablespoons freshly squeezed lemon juice

1 teaspoon finely chopped lemon zest

3 cups all-purpose flour

2 teaspoons baking powder

½ teaspoon ground mace

½ teaspoon salt

2 cups blueberries

Equipment

A 9-inch bundt pan, buttered and floured

Preheat the oven to 350 degrees.

In the bowl of an electric mixer, combine the butter, sugar, and 1 cup of the honey. Using the paddle attachment, beat the mixture on medium-high speed until light. Add the beaten eggs, 1 tablespoon of the lemon juice, and the lemon zest. Mix until smooth. Reduce to low speed and add the flour, baking powder, mace, and salt. Stir in the blueberries. Spread the batter into the prepared pan.

Bake the cake until a skewer inserted in the middle comes out clean, about 55 minutes. Cool the cake on a rack for 15 minutes and then unmold it.

In a small saucepan heat the remaining ½ cup honey and 1 tablespoon lemon juice until warm. Brush the glaze over the top and sides of the cake. Let the cake cool to room temperature.

AHEAD-OF-TIME NOTES

The cake will keep for several days. Store wrapped in plastic wrap at room temperature.

BLACKBERRY CHIFFON ROLL

This cake is so light and delicate that it seems appropriate for a white-gloved ladies' tea—but don't limit it solely to such an occasion. It's delightful anytime. Be sure to use good-quality blackberry jam.

SERVES 8

3 large eggs

¼ teaspoon vanilla extract

¼ cup plus 2 teaspoons granulated sugar

4 tablespoons (½ stick) unsalted butter, melted

¾ cup sifted all-purpose flour

½ cup blackberry jam

2 pints fresh blackberries

3 cups Whipped Cream (page 225)

Equipment

An 11½- by 13½-inch baking pan with 1-inch sides, the bottom lined with parchment paper

Preheat the oven to 375 degrees.

Fill a medium saucepan ⅓ full of water. Bring the water to a boil.

In a stainless steel bowl whisk together the eggs, vanilla, and sugar.

Set the bowl into the saucepan of boiling water, making sure the water doesn't touch the bottom of the bowl. Cook the egg mixture, whisking constantly, until the eggs are warm and the sugar is melted. Scrape the mixture into the bowl of an electric mixer. Using the whisk attachment, whip on high speed until thick and tripled in volume. With the machine running, drizzle in the melted butter and continue to whip for 1 minute. Fold in the flour. Gently spread the batter into the prepared pan.

Bake the cake until no longer wet on top, 8 to 10 minutes. With a small knife, loosen the edges of the cake from the pan. From one of the short ends, with the parchment paper still on the cake, roll the cake into a cylinder. Cool the cake.

Carefully unroll the cake. Spread the blackberry jam over the cake and reroll it, peeling off the parchment paper as you roll. Let it sit for at least 10 minutes before cutting.

With a serrated knife cut the roll into ½-inch slices. Place 3 slices of the cake on each plate, and garnish with some blackberries and whipped cream.

AHEAD-OF-TIME NOTES

The roll is best served the day it is made. Store wrapped in plastic wrap at room temperature.

GOAT CHEESE CAKE WITH MIXED BERRIES

I first served this at the first annual convention of the International Association for Women Chefs and Restaurateurs (IAWCR) in New York City. It isn't too sweet, and the goat cheese adds a savory element. It is also good after a light lunch.

SERVES 6 TO 8

11 ounces goat cheese

¾ cup granulated sugar

1 teaspoon vanilla extract

1 teaspoon freshly chopped lemon zest

1 teaspoon freshly squeezed lemon juice

6 large eggs, separated

3 tablespoons all-purpose flour

1½ pints blackberries

1½ pints raspberries

Equipment

A 9-inch round cake pan, buttered and sugared

Preheat the oven to 350 degrees.

In a medium mixing bowl, combine the goat cheese, sugar, vanilla extract, lemon zest, and lemon juice. Mix until smooth and then add the egg yolks, two at a time. Stir in the flour.

Whip the egg whites until soft peaks form. Gently fold the egg whites into the goat cheese mixture. Spread the batter into the prepared pan.

Bake the cake until a skewer inserted in the middle comes out clean, 25 to 30 minutes. Cool the cake and remove it from the pan by inverting it onto a serving platter or large plate.

Serve the goat cheese cake with the berries placed in the center of the cake.

AHEAD-OF-TIME NOTES

The cake can be made a day ahead of serving. Store at room temperature wrapped in plastic wrap. Do not add the berries until just prior to serving.

SUMMER FRUITS

♦♦♦

*Indian Free, Babcock, O'Henry peaches. Mariposa
and Santa Rosa plums. Independence apricots and Fairchild nectarines.
Take a bite out of a piece of any of these in July or August
and it bursts with juice and fragrance. Roadside stands full of ripe red
cherries — Bing, Golden Rainier, Lambert, Queen Anne.
They look so wonderful you end up buying twice the amount you need.
Your hands are stained crimson as you eat them one by one. This is fruit
at its best. Desserts made from summer's fruits should taste
as vibrant as the fruit itself. Let the flavors of the fruit stand out;
do not mask or hide them.*

CARAMELIZED RHUBARB CHARLOTTE

This is not a true charlotte because it does not have cake or bread lining the mold;
but it does have caramel. Serve with crème fraîche.

SERVES 8

½ cup water

2⅓ cups granulated sugar

1 pound 5 ounces rhubarb stalks,
   washed and trimmed

2 teaspoons finely chopped lemon zest

Large pinch of salt

5 tablespoons unsalted butter, softened

4 teaspoons all-purpose flour

4 large eggs, lightly beaten

Equipment

Eight 4-ounce ovenproof ramekins

A baking pan large enough to hold
   all the ramekins

In a small heavy-bottomed saucepan stir together the water and 1 cup of the sugar. Cook the sugar mixture over medium heat until the sugar dissolves. Increase to medium-high heat and cook until the caramel is a golden amber color. (Do not stir after you increase the heat.) Remove the caramel from the heat and pour a couple of teaspoons into one of the ramekins. Quickly swirl the ramekin so that the caramel coats the sides and bottom. Be careful —the caramel is very hot. Repeat for all the ramekins. Set them aside to harden.

Cut the rhubarb into 1-inch pieces. In a medium saucepan, combine the rhubarb, remaining 1⅓ cups sugar, lemon zest, and salt. Cook over medium heat, stirring frequently, until soft, 10 to 15 minutes.

Preheat the oven to 350 degrees.

Transfer the rhubarb to a medium mixing bowl. Cool for 10 minutes. Stir in the butter and flour. Add the beaten eggs.

Fill the caramel-lined ramekins with the rhubarb mixture. Place the ramekins in the baking pan. Carefully fill the baking pan with water so that the water reaches halfway up the sides of the ramekins.

Bake until set, about 25 minutes.

Remove the charlottes from the baking dish. Cool for 10 minutes. Run a knife around the inside edge of the ramekins and unmold onto plates and serve.

AHEAD-OF-TIME NOTES

The charlottes can be made a day in advance. Reheat for 10 minutes in a 325-degree oven. Store in the refrigerator.

BING CHERRY DUMPLINGS

Dumplings can be eaten all day—breakfast, lunch, dinner, and even in between.
The cream cheese in the dough gives the dumpling a biscuitlike texture. I prefer to serve unwhipped
heavy cream with these rather than whipped cream.

8 DUMPLINGS

Dough

8 ounces cream cheese
½ pound (2 sticks) unsalted butter, softened
1½ tablespoons granulated sugar
Pinch of salt
2 cups all-purpose flour
¾ cup heavy whipping cream

Fruit Filling

1½ pounds pitted Bing cherries
¼ cup cornstarch
1 cup granulated sugar
¼ teaspoon freshly squeezed lemon juice

Equipment

8 large muffin cups

DOUGH

In the bowl of an electric mixer, combine the cream cheese, butter, sugar, and salt. Using the paddle attachment on medium speed beat until smooth. Decrease to low speed and alternately add the flour and cream, mixing well after each addition.

Form the dough into a ball and wrap in plastic wrap and refrigerate until firm, about 30 minutes. On a lightly floured work surface roll the dough ¼ inch thick. Cut the dough into 5-inch squares. Reroll the scraps of dough as necessary until there are 8 squares. Press the squares into the muffin cups, letting the corners of the dough hang over the sides. Set aside.

Preheat the oven to 325 degrees.

FRUIT FILLING

In a medium bowl, mix together the cherries, cornstarch, sugar and lemon juice. Fill each muffin cup with about ½ cup of the cherry filling.

Bake until golden brown, about 45 minutes. Cool for 5 minutes and then remove the dumplings from the muffin cups with a large spoon.

AHEAD-OF-TIME NOTES

The dumplings are best eaten the day they are baked. The dough can be made and rolled a day ahead. Store in the refrigerator wrapped in plastic wrap.

BAKED APRICOTS WITH VANILLA ICE CREAM AND ALMOND PRALINE

Baking fruit helps bring out its delicate aromas and perfumes. Any stone fruit can be used in this recipe; just be careful to choose fruit that is ripe but still firm or it will become mushy when baked.

SERVES 6

¾ cup firmly packed dark brown sugar

4 tablespoons (½ stick) unsalted butter, softened

Pinch of salt

Pinch of ground nutmeg

Pinch of ground cinnamon

½ cup water

½ cup granulated sugar

9 ripe firm apricots

6 scoops Vanilla Ice Cream (page 240)

½ cup Almond Praline (page 217)

Equipment

A medium-sized baking dish large enough to hold the apricots in a single layer

Preheat the oven to 350 degrees.

In a small bowl, mix together the brown sugar, butter, salt, nutmeg, and cinnamon. Set aside.

In a small saucepan stir together the water and the sugar. Over high heat, bring the mixture to a boil. Let the sugar mixture boil until the sugar dissolves, about 1 minute. Pour the syrup into the baking dish.

Cut the apricots in half and discard the pits. Place the apricots in the baking dish cut side up. Dab the brown sugar butter mixture on top of the apricots.

Bake until soft, about 15 minutes. Serve the apricots warm, 3 halves to a plate, with the vanilla ice cream and a sprinkle of the almond praline.

AHEAD-OF-TIME NOTES

The baked apricots should be eaten warm from the oven.

PEACH SHERBET

When I was a child we always made peach sherbet in the summer. We had a hand-crank ice cream maker that you layered with ice and salt. As the youngest in my family, I didn't usually have to take a turn cranking the ice cream. However, I still had to wait for it to freeze—it seemed like eternity!

2 QUARTS

4 pounds very ripe peaches

2 cups granulated sugar

2 cups water

1½ cups milk

½ teaspoon vanilla extract

Pinch of salt

Halve the peaches. Leave the skins on and remove the pits.

Put the peaches in a large saucepan with the sugar and water. Cook over medium-high heat until soft, about 10 minutes. Purée the peaches and their liquid and cool to room temperature. Stir in the milk, vanilla, and salt.

Freeze in an ice cream machine according to manufacturer's instructions.

AHEAD-OF-TIME NOTES

The sherbet can be made a day in advance.

PATRICK'S PEACH PIE

I call this Patrick's peach pie because every year he is one of the first people who asks me when peaches will be available and will I please make him a pie. Patrick is my peach barometer; when he starts asking about peach pie I know that the season is just about to begin.

A 9-INCH PIE

3 pounds ripe, firm peaches
¼ cup firmly packed brown sugar
¾ cup granulated sugar
¼ cup cornstarch
¼ teaspoon grated nutmeg
¾ teaspoon ground cinnamon
Pinch of salt
1 large egg, lightly beaten

1 prebaked pie shell (page 226)
Lattice for one pie (page 226)

Preheat the oven to 350 degrees.

Peel, pit, and slice the peaches ¾ inch thick. Place the peaches in a medium mixing bowl.

In a small bowl, mix together the brown and granulated sugars, the cornstarch, nutmeg, cinnamon, and salt. Gently stir the spice mixture into the peaches. Place the peach mixture in the prebaked pie shell. Brush the beaten egg on the lattice. Lay the lattice over the top of the pie in a crisscross pattern.

Bake the pie until the juices have thickened, about 1 hour. If the crust gets brown before the pie has finished baking, cover it loosely with aluminum foil.

AHEAD-OF-TIME NOTES

Peach pie is best eaten the day it is made.

PISTACHIO ICE CREAM WITH A PEACH COMPOTE

Pistachios are the best type of nuts to serve with peaches. Both have intense, concentrated flavors.

SERVES 6

Pistachio Ice Cream

3 cups (12 ounces) pistachios, toasted

1⅓ cups granulated sugar

12 large egg yolks

½ teaspoon salt

3 cups milk

3½ cups heavy whipping cream

Peach Compote

1¼ pounds ripe peaches

1 tablespoon unsalted butter

2 tablespoons firmly packed dark brown sugar

1 teaspoon freshly squeezed lemon juice

PISTACHIO ICE CREAM

Coarsely chop 1 cup of the pistachios. Set aside for the garnish. In a food processor finely grind the remaining pistachios with the sugar.

In a medium mixing bowl, stir together the pistachio sugar, egg yolks, and salt.

In a heavy-bottomed saucepan, scald the milk and the heavy cream over medium heat. Whisk the milk mixture into the pistachio mixture. Return the mixture to the saucepan and cook over medium heat, stirring constantly until it coats the back of a spoon, about 5 minutes. Refrigerate the ice cream base until cold. Strain the liquid through a medium sieve, discarding the pistachios.

Freeze the ice cream in an ice cream machine according to machine manufacturer's instructions. When the ice cream is frozen, fold in the coarsely chopped pistachios.

PEACH COMPOTE

Peel, pit, and slice the peaches ¼ inch thick. Melt the butter in a large sauté pan over medium high heat. Stir in the brown sugar and lemon juice. Add the peaches and cook just until the peaches are warmed through, about 3 minutes.

Immediately spoon the warm peaches over the pistachio ice cream and serve at once.

AHEAD-OF-TIME NOTES

The ice cream can be made several days in advance. The compote should be made at the last minute.

PEACH BLACKBERRY COBBLER

The first time I made this recipe I used peaches and blackberries from the very first crop in my orchard!
It was exciting to be able to bake with fruit I had grown myself.
The fruit was picked in the late afternoon, the cobbler was baked, and within a half hour
it was all eaten! Serve warm with Vanilla Ice Cream (page 240).

SERVES 8

Cobbler Topping

8 tablespoons (1 stick) unsalted cold butter

¼ cup all-purpose flour

¼ cup cornmeal

2 tablespoons granulated sugar

Pinch of salt

1 or 2 tablespoons ice water

Fruit Filling

1¼ pounds ripe peaches

½ pint blackberries

¾ cup granulated sugar

3 tablespoons cornstarch

¼ teaspoon ground mace

Pinch of salt

4 tablespoons (½ stick) unsalted butter, melted

1 large egg, slightly beaten

Equipment

A 1½-quart shallow ovenproof dish

COBBLER TOPPING

In the bowl of an electric mixer, combine the butter, flour, cornmeal, sugar, and salt. With the paddle attachment mix on low speed until the butter is the size of small peas. Slowly add just enough ice water so the mixture is no longer dry. Mix just until combined.

On a lightly floured work surface, roll the dough ⅜ inch thick. Cut the dough into circles or any decorative shape that you like. Refrigerate until firm, about 30 minutes.

FRUIT FILLING

Preheat the oven to 350 degrees.

Peel, pit, and slice the peaches ¾ inch thick. In a medium bowl, combine the peaches and blackberries. Mix in the sugar, cornstarch, mace, and salt. Put the peach mixture in the ovenproof dish. Drizzle the melted butter over the peach mixture.

Place the refrigerated dough on top of the peaches. Brush the beaten egg over the dough. Bake until the top is golden brown and the peach mixture has thickened, about 40 minutes.

AHEAD-OF-TIME NOTES

The cobbler is best eaten the day it is baked. It can be reheated. Store at room temperature.

CHERRIES JUBILEE WITH ALMOND ICE CREAM

A popular dessert of the 1950s and early 1960s, cherries jubilee seems to have lost its popularity.
It has, however, all the elements of a good dessert—fresh fruit, ice cream, and the contrast of hot and cold.
(I have left out the step where the dessert is flamed at the table!)

SERVES 6

1 pound fresh cherries, preferably Bing

½ cup granulated sugar

1 tablespoon freshly squeezed lemon juice

2 tablespoons kirsch or brandy

1 tablespoon unsalted butter, softened

6 scoops of Almond Ice Cream (page 240)

Pit and halve the cherries.

Place the pitted cherries and the sugar in a large sauté pan. Cook over medium heat until they begin to give off a little juice, 3 to 5 minutes. Stir in the lemon juice, kirsch or brandy, and boil for 1 minute. Remove from the heat and stir in the butter. Put the almond ice cream into 6 bowls. Pour the cherries and some sauce over the ice cream. Serve immediately.

AHEAD-OF-TIME NOTES

This dessert should be made at the last minute.

PEACH BLUEBERRY BROWN BETTY

A brown Betty is fruit that is layered with bread and then baked. I like to use brioche because of its buttery flavor. Serve warm with Half-whipped Cream (page 225) or crème fraîche.

SERVES 8

1 pound brioche or other rich egg bread

12 tablespoons (1½ sticks) unsalted butter, melted

1¼ cups granulated sugar

1 tablespoon ground cinnamon

½ teaspoon grated nutmeg

2 tablespoons all-purpose flour

1¼ pounds ripe peaches

1½ pints blueberries

3 tablespoons cornstarch

¼ cup firmly packed dark brown sugar

Equipment

An ovenproof pan, 9 by 13 inches

Preheat the oven to 350 degrees.

Trim the crust from the brioche and cut the brioche into ¾-inch cubes. Place the cubes on a baking sheet and bake until light brown, about 10 minutes.

In a medium bowl combine the bread cubes and the melted butter and mix until combined. Add 1 cup of the sugar, the cinnamon, nutmeg, and flour. Mix until the bread cubes are well coated. Place half of the bread cubes in the bottom of the baking dish.

Peel, pit, and slice the peaches ¼ inch thick. In a medium bowl combine the peaches, blueberries, cornstarch, brown sugar and remaining ¾ cup granulated sugar. Mix until combined. Place the fruit mixture in the baking dish over the bread cubes. Top with the remaining bread cubes. Bake until the brioche is brown and the fruit is bubbling, 35 to 40 minutes. Serve warm.

AHEAD-OF-TIME NOTES

The brown Betty is best eaten the day it is baked. It can be reheated.

FROZEN PEACH MOUSSE WITH RASPBERRY PURÉE

Like ice cream but (believe it or not!) richer and creamier.
If you like, this can also be made in one large mold. Garnish with fresh sliced peaches.

SERVES 8

1 pound ripe peaches

3 large egg yolks

⅓ cup Sugar Syrup (page 239)

Pinch of salt

⅔ cup heavy whipping cream

1½ cups sweetened Raspberry Purée (page 238)

Equipment

Eight 4-ounce molds

Halve and pit the peaches. Purée them through a food mill or in a food processor. Strain the purée through a medium sieve to eliminate the skin. Set aside.

Fill a medium saucepan ⅓ full of water. Bring the water to a simmer over medium heat.

In a medium stainless steel mixing bowl, whisk together the yolks, the sugar syrup, and salt. Set the bowl into the pot of boiling water. Make sure the bowl fits snugly in the pot; at the same time, the bottom of the bowl should not touch the water. The bowl mustn't be too deep nor the water level too high. Cook the mixture, whisking constantly until thick, 2 to 3 minutes. Remove the bowl from the heat and whisk until the egg mixture is at room temperature. Fold in the peach purée.

In a medium mixing bowl, whip the cream until soft peaks form. Fold the cream into the peach mixture. Divide the peach mixture among the eight molds. Freeze until hard, 2 to 3 hours.

Unmold the frozen peach mousses and place them on plates. Spoon some raspberry purée around the plates.

AHEAD-OF-TIME NOTES

The mousse can be made a day in advance.

HAZELNUT SHORTCAKES WITH A PLUM COMPOTE

Shortcakes are best eaten the day they are made because that is when they have the lightest texture. Served with warm fruit, they melt in your mouth.

SERVES 6

Shortcakes

¾ cup (3 ounces) hazelnuts, toasted and skinned

⅓ cup plus 1 teaspoon granulated sugar

2 cups all-purpose flour

½ teaspoon salt

1 tablespoon baking powder

8 tablespoons (1 stick) unsalted cold butter

½ cup plus 2 tablespoons heavy whipping cream

Plum Compote

1½ pounds (about 7) ripe plums

¾ cups granulated sugar

2 teaspoons freshly squeezed lemon juice

3 tablespoons unsalted butter

3 cups Whipped Cream (page 225)

SHORTCAKES

Preheat the oven to 350 degrees.

In a food processor, coarsely grind the hazelnuts and ⅓ cup sugar.

In a medium bowl, combine the hazelnut mixture, flour, salt, baking powder, and butter. With a pastry blender mix the ingredients until the butter is the size of small peas. Slowly pour in ½ cup plus 1 tablespoon of cream and mix just until the dough comes together.

On a lightly floured work surface, pat or roll the dough 1 inch thick and cut into six 2½-inch-wide circles. Place the shortcakes on a baking tray. Brush the tops with the remaining tablespoon of cream. Sprinkle with the remaining teaspoon sugar. Bake until golden brown, about 35 minutes.

PLUM COMPOTE

Slice the plums ½ inch thick. In a large sauté pan, combine the plums, sugar, and lemon juice. Cook over medium heat until the sugar is dissolved. Stir in the butter and cook until the sauce thickens slightly, 1 to 2 minutes.

Split the shortcakes in half horizontally and place the bottom of each shortcake on a plate. Cover the shortcake with some whipped cream and some of the plums. Top with the second half of the shortcake.

AHEAD-OF-TIME NOTES

Bake the shortcakes the day you plan to serve them. The plum compote is best prepared at the last minute.

APRICOT CUSTARD TART

This is one of my favorite summertime desserts. It is ideal after a dinner of barbecued chicken, sliced tomatoes, and fresh corn on the cob.

SERVES 6 TO 8

13 ounces (about 5) ripe apricots

1 prebaked 9½-inch tart shell (page 226)

1 cup granulated sugar

2 large egg yolks

¾ cup heavy cream

2 tablespoons all-purpose flour

Pinch of salt

¼ cup (1 ounce) sliced almonds

Preheat the oven to 325 degrees.

Slice the apricots ¾ inch thick, discarding the pits. Place the apricots in the prebaked tart shell in a decorative pattern. Set aside.

Combine the sugar, egg yolks, and cream in a medium mixing bowl. Whisk until combined. Stir in the flour and salt. Carefully pour the creamy mixture over the apricots.

Sprinkle the almonds over the top of the tart. Bake until the custard is almost completely set, about 35 to 40 minutes. Serve slightly warm or at room temperature.

AHEAD-OF-TIME NOTES

The tart is best served the day it is made.

SPICED RHUBARB HAZELNUT TART

Cinnamon and ginger are a natural combination with rhubarb; as rhubarb is so strong it needs other flavors to help balance it. Serve with Almond Ice Cream (page 241) or whipped cream.

SERVES 6

Crust

1⅔ cups (6½ ounces) hazelnuts, toasted and skinned

½ cup granulated sugar

½ pound (2 sticks) unsalted butter, softened

2 large egg yolks

½ teaspoon ground cinnamon

¼ teaspoon ground ginger

Pinch of salt

1¼ cups all-purpose flour

Rhubarb Filling

2 pounds rhubarb, washed and trimmed

1 teaspoon finely chopped lemon zest

3 cups granulated sugar

¼ cup water

Equipment

A 9½-inch tart pan

CRUST

In a food processor finely grind the hazelnuts and sugar.

In the bowl of an electric mixer, combine the hazelnut mixture and butter. Using the paddle attachment, mix the ingredients on medium low speed until soft. Add the egg yolks. Decrease to low speed, and add the cinnamon, ginger, salt, and flour. Mix until combined. Chill the dough until firm, about 30 minutes.

Place the dough on a lightly floured work surface. Roll ⅓ of the dough ³⁄₁₆ inch thick. Cut it into ½-inch strips. Roll the remaining dough ⅛ inch thick. Line the tart shell with the dough. Chill the tart shell and the lattice for at least 1 hour.

RHUBARB FILLING

Cut the rhubarb into ½-inch pieces. In a large saucepan combine the rhubarb, lemon zest, sugar, and water. Cook over medium heat, stirring occasionally, until soft, 10 to 15 minutes. Strain off any watery liquid and discard it. Let the rhubarb cool to room temperature.

Preheat the oven to 350 degrees.

Spread the rhubarb purée in the tart shell. Cover the tart with the lattice in a crisscross pattern. Bake until brown, about 55 minutes.

AHEAD-OF-TIME NOTES

The tart shell can be prepared several days in advance and frozen. The rhubarb filling can be made a day in advance. The tart is at its best if eaten the same day it is baked.

RHUBARB UPSIDE-DOWN CAKE

As my brother-in-law will attest, even nonrhubarb lovers like this cake.
Serve with whipped cream or crème fraîche.

SERVES 8 TO 10

1¼ pounds rhubarb, cleaned and trimmed

1 cup granulated sugar

1¾ cups sifted cake flour

1½ teaspoons baking powder

¼ teaspoon salt

¾ teaspoon ground cinnamon

½ teaspoon ground ginger

⅛ teaspoon ground cloves

8 tablespoons (1 stick) unsalted butter,
    softened

¾ cup firmly packed dark brown sugar

2 teaspoons vanilla extract

¾ cup milk

4 large egg whites

Equipment

A 9-inch round by 3-inch high cake pan,
    the bottom lined with parchment paper

Preheat the oven to 325 degrees.

Cut the rhubarb into ¾-inch pieces. In a medium-sized bowl combine the rhubarb and ¾ cup of the granulated sugar. Spread the rhubarb in the bottom of the cake pan. Set aside.

Sift together the cake flour, baking powder, salt, cinnamon, ginger, and cloves. Set aside.

In the bowl of an electric mixer combine the butter and brown sugar. Using the paddle attachment, beat on medium speed until light. Add the vanilla extract to the milk. Decrease to low speed and alternately add the dry ingredients and milk. Once all the ingredients have been added, increase to medium speed and beat the mixture for 2 minutes.

In a clean bowl of an electric mixer using the whisk attachment, whip the egg whites on medium speed until frothy. Increase to high speed, slowly add the remaining sugar and whisk until soft peaks form. Gently fold the egg whites into the cake batter. Spread the batter over the rhubarb.

Bake until a skewer inserted in the middle comes out clean, about 1 hour and 10 minutes. Let cool for 20 minutes. Run a knife around the inside edge of the pan, invert the cake onto a serving platter, and remove the parchment paper.

AHEAD-OF-TIME NOTES

The cake can be made a day in advance, but it will taste the best the day it is baked. Store wrapped in plastic wrap at room temperature.

PLUM VANILLA BOMBE
WITH PLUM CARAMEL SAUCE

Like a creamsicle in texture, this is a real summertime refresher. Try to use red plums in this recipe, as they yield a beautiful red-pink color.

SERVES 8 TO 10

2 pounds ripe plums

¾ cup Sugar Syrup (page 239)

Large pinch of salt

1 teaspoon freshly squeezed lemon juice

1 quart Vanilla Ice Cream (page 240)

3 cups Plum Caramel Sauce (page 228)

Equipment

A terrine pan 12 by 4 by 3½ inches, lined with plastic wrap

Cut the plums in half and discard the pits. In a food processor purée the plums. Strain the purée through a medium sieve to eliminate any pieces of skin. There should be about 2½ cups of purée.

Combine the plum purée, sugar syrup, salt, and lemon juice in a bowl. Mix until combined.

Freeze the sorbet in an ice cream machine according to machine manufacturer's instructions.

Press half of the plum sorbet firmly in the bottom of the terrine pan. Freeze until firm, about 30 minutes. Put half of the vanilla ice cream on top of the plum sorbet, pressing down firmly. Again freeze until firm. Make two more layers with the remaining plum sorbet and vanilla ice cream. Freeze the terrine for several hours until frozen.

To unmold the terrine, invert it and remove the pan. Peel off the plastic wrap. Slice the terrine with a sharp knife. Serve with the plum caramel sauce.

AHEAD-OF-TIME NOTES

The bombe can be prepared several days in advance, and can be sliced in advance. Wrap the individual slices in parchment paper.

NECTARINE BLUEBERRY CRISP

Summer wouldn't be complete without one, if not several, crisps. Adjust the fruit combinations as you desire. Serve with Half-whipped Cream (page 225) or crème fraîche.

SERVES 6

3 pounds ripe nectarines

2½ cups blueberries

2 teaspoons freshly squeezed lemon juice

½ cup granulated sugar

1 cup plus 2 tablespoons all-purpose flour

Pinch of salt

½ cup firmly packed dark brown sugar

8 tablespoons (1 stick) unsalted cold butter

2 teaspoons finely chopped lemon zest

Equipment

A 2-quart ovenproof baking dish

Preheat the oven to 350 degrees

Halve and pit the nectarines. Slice them ½ inch thick.

In a large mixing bowl, combine the nectarines, blueberries, lemon juice, sugar, 2 tablespoons of flour, and salt. Place the mixture in the baking dish.

In a food processor, combine the remaining 1 cup flour, dark brown sugar, butter, and lemon zest. Using quick on-off turns, process the mixture until the butter is the size of small peas. Sprinkle the streusel over the fruit mixture.

Bake until the fruit juices are bubbling and the streusel is nicely browned, 30 to 35 minutes. Serve the crisp warm.

AHEAD-OF-TIME NOTES

The crisp is best eaten the day it is made. It can be reheated.

PEACH FRANGIPANE TART

This is a wonderful tart to take to a picnic. It doesn't need to be refrigerated, is attractive with the frangipane layer, and is good as is, without any sauces, making transportation simple.

SERVES 6 TO 8

1 cup (4 ounces) almonds,
   toasted and coarsely chopped

4 tablespoons (½ stick) unsalted butter,
   softened, plus 4 tablespoons (½ stick)
   unsalted butter, melted

⅓ cup plus 1 tablespoon granulated sugar

1 large egg

1 prebaked 9½-inch tart shell (page 226)

4 ripe peaches

1 teaspoon lemon juice

Preheat the oven to 350 degrees.

In the bowl of an electric mixer, combine the almonds, the 4 tablespoons softened butter, and ⅓ cup of the sugar. Using the paddle attachment, beat for 2 minutes on medium speed. Add the egg and mix for 1 minute. Spread the almond frangipane in the bottom of the prebaked tart shell.

Peel, pit, and slice the peaches ¼ inch thick. Arrange the peaches in a circular pattern on top of the almond frangipane.

In a small bowl combine the 1 remaining table-spoon sugar, the lemon juice, and the 4 tablespoons melted butter. Brush half of the mixture over the peaches.

Bake until the frangipane is set, 15 to 20 minutes. Brush the remaining butter-sugar mixture over the top of the tart. Let cool for at least 10 minutes before slicing.

Serve the tart warm or at room temperature.

AHEAD-OF-TIME NOTES

The tart is best served the day it is made. Store at room temperature.

TIPSY ITALIAN NECTARINES

Fresh tree-ripened nectarines are marinated in Moscato d'Asti, a light sparkling Italian dessert wine,
and filled with a hazelnut cream. A very light and simple-to-prepare dessert.
If you wish, you can serve it with sweetened Raspberry Purée (page 238) on the side.

SERVES 6

Nectarines

6 large ripe nectarines

2 cups Moscato d'Asti

¼ cup Sugar Syrup (page 239)

Hazelnut Cream

¼ cup (1 ounce) hazelnuts,
    toasted and skinned

½ cup heavy whipping cream

1 tablespoon sour cream

2 teaspoons granulated sugar

NECTARINES

Slice off the very top of the nectarines. Insert a paring knife in one of the nectarines against the pit. Gently carve around the pit, loosening it from the flesh. Press the knife against the bottom of the pit and gently push it out of the nectarine, keeping the nectarine whole. Remove the pits from the other nectarines in the same manner.

In a large mixing bowl combine the Moscato d'Asti and sugar syrup. Place the nectarines in the liquid and marinate for 1 hour.

HAZELNUT CREAM

Coarsely chop the hazelnuts.

In a medium mixing bowl, combine the cream, sour cream and sugar. Whip until soft peaks form. Fold in the hazelnuts.

FINISHING

Remove the nectarines from the marinating liquid. Shave ⅛ inch off the bottoms of the nectarines so that they stand up. Place each nectarine on a plate. Fill the nectarines with the hazelnut cream. Serve immediately.

AHEAD-OF-TIME NOTES

The nectarines can marinate in the Moscato d'Asti for several hours. Fill them with the cream just before serving.

YELLOW AND RED WATERMELON ICES

I like to buy whole watermelons instead of the already cut pieces in the grocery store because a watermelon is best as soon as it is cut. Often, once you get home, you find out you have too much watermelon to eat by the slice. Here's a solution to that problem.

ABOUT 2 QUARTS

1½ pounds red watermelon, rind removed

1½ pounds yellow watermelon,
  rind removed

1 cup granulated sugar

2 teaspoons freshly squeezed lime juice

Pinch of salt

Coarsely cut the flesh of the red and yellow watermelons, keeping the two types separate. Remove any seeds. In a food processor, separately purée each of the watermelons until smooth. Strain the purées through a medium sieve. There should be about 2 cups of each purée.

Stir ½ cup of sugar, 1 teaspoon of lime juice, and a pinch of salt into each of the watermelon purées. If the watermelon isn't very sweet, add a little more sugar. Pour the purées into two shallow pans. Freeze the mixtures, stirring every half hour, until hard. (Stirring the ices during freezing improves the texture of the ice.)

To serve, spoon some of each ice into bowls.

AHEAD-OF-TIME NOTES

The ices will last for several days. If they sit overnight and freeze in a solid block, break them up with a fork to regain their light feathery texture.

MOLASSES CAKE
WITH PLUM RASPBERRY COMPOTE

Like gingerbread but with more molasses flavor. Serve with Half-whipped Cream (page 225).

SERVES 8

Molasses Cake

2 cups all-purpose flour

¼ teaspoon salt

½ teaspoon ground cinnamon

1 cup molasses

1 teaspoon baking soda

8 tablespoons (1 stick) unsalted butter, softened

1 cup firmly packed brown sugar

2 large eggs, separated

1 teaspoon vanilla extract

½ cup heavy cream

Plum Raspberry Compote

½ cup freshly squeezed orange juice

1 tablespoon Grand Marnier

½ teaspoon freshly squeezed lemon juice

4 teaspoons granulated sugar

6 ripe plums, sliced ¼ inch thick

2 tablespoons unsalted butter

1 pint raspberries

Equipment

An 8- by 8-inch pan, buttered and floured

MOLASSES CAKE

Preheat the oven to 350 degrees.

Sift together the flour, salt, and cinnamon. Set aside.

In a small bowl, combine the molasses and the baking soda. Set aside.

In the bowl of an electric mixer, combine the butter and the brown sugar. Using the paddle attachment, beat on medium-high speed until smooth. Add the egg yolks one at a time and beat well. Add the molasses mixture. Add the vanilla to the cream. Decrease to low speed and alternately add the flour mixture and the cream.

In a clean bowl, whip the egg whites until soft peaks form. Fold them into the batter.

Gently spread the batter into the prepared cake pan. Bake the cake until a skewer inserted in the middle comes out clean, 45 to 50 minutes.

Cool the cake to room temperature.

PLUM RASPBERRY COMPOTE

In a large sauté pan over medium high heat, cook the orange juice, Grand Marnier, lemon juice, and sugar for 1 to 2 minutes. Add the plums and the butter and cook 2 or 3 minutes more. Remove the pan from the heat and gently stir in the raspberries. Immediately serve the compote with a piece of the molasses cake.

AHEAD-OF-TIME NOTES

The molasses cake can be made a day in advance. Store wrapped in plastic wrap at room temperature. The plum raspberry compote should be made at the last minute.

PLUM BISCUITS

Serve these as part of a weekend breakfast buffet with Brown Sugar
Crème Fraîche (page 236). The dough can be made at night and the biscuits can be baked first thing
in the morning so they will be nice and fresh.

SERVES 8

2½ cups all-purpose flour

½ teaspoon baking powder

½ teaspoon salt

6 ounces cream cheese

½ pound (2 sticks) unsalted butter, softened

¼ cup granulated sugar

2 teaspoons finely chopped lemon zest

3 ripe firm plums, pitted

Preheat the oven to 350 degrees.

Sift together the flour, baking powder, and the salt. Set aside.

In the bowl of an electric mixer combine the cream cheese, butter, sugar, and lemon zest. Using the paddle attachment on medium speed, beat the mixture until smooth.

Cut the plums into ⅜-inch pieces. Set the mixer at low speed and add the plum pieces to the cream cheese mixture. Stir in the flour mixture and mix just until the dough comes together.

Lightly flour a work surface and the top of the dough. Pat the dough 1¼ inches thick. Cut the biscuits into 2½-inch shapes. Place the biscuits on a baking tray.

Bake until golden brown, 25 to 30 minutes.

AHEAD-OF-TIME NOTES

The biscuits are best served warm from the oven.

FALL FRUITS, DRIED FRUITS, AND NUTS

♦♦♦

When I think of what to make in the fall for dessert
my first thoughts are of caramel and warm desserts. Caramel's beautiful
shade of amber, much like fall itself, naturally pairs with apples,
pears, pumpkins, figs, cranberries, and nuts — all the fruits one associates
with this season. Such warm desserts as pear chausson fresh
from the oven or honey marsala baked figs with a ginger sabayon help
fight the chill in the air.

TOASTED ALMOND SOUR CHERRY STRUDEL

This is not a classic strudel, since it doesn't call for the traditional strudel dough, but filo makes it easier to prepare. Serve with Half-whipped Cream (page 225).

SERVES 6 TO 8

2 cups dried sour cherries

1¼ cups granulated sugar

½ cup water

¼ cup honey

2½ cups (10 ounces) sliced almonds, toasted

1 teaspoon ground cinnamon

8 sheets of filo

6 tablespoons (¾ stick) unsalted butter, melted

In a medium saucepan combine the cherries, ¾ cup of sugar, the water, and honey. Cook over medium heat until slightly syrupy. Remove from the heat and stir in the almonds. Set aside to cool.

In a small bowl, mix the remaining ½ cup sugar with the cinnamon.

Stack the sheets of filo and keep covered with a damp towel. Remove one sheet and place it lengthwise on the work surface. Brush the sheet with some melted butter and sprinkle 2 teaspoons of the sugar mixture on top. Place a second sheet of filo on top of the first. Butter and sugar it. Continue stacking, buttering and sprinkling until there are four layers of filo.

Using the remaining sheets of filo, make a second stack of filo layers in the same manner.

Preheat the oven to 350 degrees.

Spread the cherry almond mixture over one of the stacks of filo leaving a ½-inch edge on all sides. Carefully lift and place the second stack of filo on top of the cherry almond mixture. From one of the short ends, roll the filo into a cylinder. Tuck the ends of the roll under the bottom. Brush the top with any remaining butter and sprinkle any leftover cinnamon sugar on top. Bake until golden brown, 15 to 20 minutes. Slice and serve warm.

AHEAD-OF-TIME NOTES

The strudel is best eaten the day it is made.
Store wrapped in plastic wrap at room temperature.

ALMOND CAKE WITH AN APRICOT AND SOUR CHERRY COMPOTE

This cake can be served by itself for breakfast or as a midafternoon snack.
With the addition of fruit, it is turned into a sophisticated dessert. I like to make it in a loaf pan,
but you can also use a bundt pan or a round cake pan.

SERVES 8

Almond Cake

1¼ cups all-purpose flour

½ teaspoon baking powder

⅛ teaspoon salt

10 tablespoons (1¼ stick) unsalted butter,
    softened

5 ounces almond paste

¾ cup granulated sugar

3 large eggs

½ teaspoon almond extract

Apricot and Sour Cherry Compote

1½ cups dried apricots

1½ cups dried cherries

1½ cups granulated sugar

3 cups water

¼ cup brandy

2 tablespoons freshly squeezed lemon juice

Equipment

A 12- by 4½-inch loaf pan,
    buttered and floured

ALMOND CAKE

Preheat the oven to 325 degrees.

Sift together the flour, baking powder, and salt. Set aside.

In the bowl of an electric mixer combine the butter, almond paste, and sugar. Using the paddle attachment, beat the mixture on medium speed until well combined. Add the eggs one at a time. Reduce to low speed and add the almond extract. Stir in the reserved dry ingredients.

Spread the batter in the prepared pan and bake until a skewer inserted in the middle comes out clean, 35 to 40 minutes. Cool the cake and then unmold it.

APRICOT AND SOUR CHERRY COMPOTE

Combine the apricots, cherries, sugar, and water in a medium saucepan. Cook over medium heat until almost all the liquid has been absorbed, about 10 to 15 minutes. Stir in the brandy and lemon juice.

The compote can be served warm or at room temperature with the almond cake.

AHEAD-OF-TIME NOTES

The cake and the compote can both be made a day in advance.

CARAMELIZED CRANBERRY TART

This is a wonderful and colorful holiday dessert. Serve it with Orange Honey Ice Cream (page 242) or the Candied Cranberry Clusters (page 200).

SERVES 6 TO 8

1¼ *cups heavy whipping cream*

1½ *cups granulated sugar*

⅓ *cup water*

2 *cups cranberries*

2 *large eggs, lightly beaten*

¾ *teaspoon finely chopped orange zest*

Equipment

A 9½-inch prebaked tart shell (page 226)

Preheat the oven to 325 degrees.

In a small saucepan, scald the cream over medium-high heat. Remove the cream from the heat and cover. Set aside.

In a medium saucepan, stir together the sugar and the water. Cook over medium heat until the sugar dissolves. Increase to high heat and cook the sugar until it is golden amber in color. (Do not stir after you increase the heat.) Remove the saucepan from the stove and slowly add half the cranberries, stirring them until they release their juice and wilt slightly.

Slowly add the warm cream, stirring constantly. Stir in the remaining cranberries. Cool for 5 minutes and then whisk in the eggs and the orange zest. Mix until incorporated.

Pour the mixture into the prebaked pie shell. Bake until thick and bubbly, about 1 hour. Cool the tart before cutting.

AHEAD-OF-TIME NOTES

The tart is best served the day it is baked.

PEAR PECAN NAPOLEON

Pears and ground pecans are layered between sheets of flaky puff pastry to create a delicate
and flavorful dessert. Eat this dessert within a few hours of assembling it so the puff pastry remains crisp.
Serve with Vanilla Crème Anglaise (page 232).

SERVES 6

Pears

6 pears, peeled, cored,
   and sliced ¼ inch thick

⅔ cup granulated sugar

1 tablespoon freshly squeezed lemon juice

Pinch of salt

1 teaspoon ground cinnamon

Pecan Paste

2 cups (8 ounces) pecans, toasted

2 tablespoons granulated sugar

2 tablespoons water

1½ teaspoons finely chopped orange zest

Pinch of salt

1 pound Puff Pastry (page 234)

PEARS

Place the pears, sugar, lemon juice, salt, and cinnamon in a large sauté pan. Cook over medium-high heat, stirring occasionally, until the pears are soft and most of the liquid has evaporated, 10 to 15 minutes. Let cool.

PECAN PASTE

In a food processor, finely grind the pecans and granulated sugar. Place the pecan mixture in a small bowl and add the water, orange zest, and salt. Mix just until combined.

PUFF PASTRY

On a lightly floured work surface, roll the piece of puff pastry into a 16-inch square. Cut into 4 rectangles, each 4 inches wide by 16 inches long. With a fork, pierce small holes all over the pastry. Place the rectangles on two baking sheets. Freeze or refrigerate until firm.

Preheat the oven to 375 degrees.

Place a second baking sheet or an inverted wire mesh rack on top of the puff pastry to prevent it from rising as it bakes. Bake until golden brown, 10 to 15 minutes. Cool to room temperature.

(continued)

For Assembly

1 teaspoon granulated sugar
¼ teaspoon ground cinnamon

ASSEMBLY

Spread ⅓ of the pecan paste on one of the rectangles of puff pastry. Carefully layer ⅓ of the pears over the pecan paste. Layer two more pieces of pastry with the remaining pecan paste and pears in the same manner. Using a wide metal spatula, carefully stack these three pieces of pastry.

In a small bowl mix together the sugar and the cinnamon. Dust the fourth piece of puff pastry with the cinnamon sugar and place it on top of the stacked layers of pastry.

Using a serrated knife and a gentle sawing motion, trim the edges of the napoleon so that they are even. In the same manner, cut the napoleon into 8 pieces and serve a portion on each of 8 plates.

AHEAD-OF-TIME NOTES

The puff pastry can be made ahead and frozen in advance. Bake the pastry and make the pecan paste the day you plan to serve the dessert. The pear purée can be made several days in advance. Store the pear pecan napoleon at room temperature.

SPICED CHEESECAKE WITH A WALNUT CRUST

Most cheesecakes can be served by themselves without embellishments; this one is no exception.

SERVES 8 TO 10

Walnut Crust

2 cups (8 ounces) walnuts, toasted

1 tablespoon granulated sugar

3 tablespoons unsalted butter, melted

Spiced Filling

2 pounds cream cheese

1 cup mascarpone

1¼ cups granulated sugar

2 large eggs

Pinch of salt

1 teaspoon freshly squeezed lemon juice

⅛ teaspoon ground cloves

¼ teaspoon grated nutmeg

Equipment

A 9-inch springform pan

A baking pan large enough to hold the springform pan

WALNUT CRUST

Preheat the oven to 325 degrees.

Wrap the bottom and sides of the springform pan tightly in aluminum foil.

In a food processor, finely grind the walnuts and the sugar.

In a mixing bowl, stir together the walnut mixture and the melted butter. Press this crust into the bottom of the springform pan. Bake until dry, 10 to 15 minutes. Cool the crust to room temperature.

SPICED FILLING

In the bowl of an electric mixer combine the cream cheese, mascarpone, and sugar. On medium speed, using the paddle attachment, beat until smooth. Add the eggs, salt, lemon juice, cloves, and nutmeg. Mix until well combined. Spread the filling over the crust in the springform pan.

Place the cheesecake in the large baking pan. Place the baking pan on a rack in the middle of the oven. Fill the baking pan with water so that the water comes about halfway up the sides of the baking pan. Bake until all but the center of the cheesecake is set, 45 to 55 minutes.

Carefully remove the cheesecake from the larger baking pan and run a knife around the inside edge of the cheesecake pan. (This will prevent the cheesecake from sticking to the pan as it cools, causing cracks in the middle of the cheesecake.) Cool to room temperature and then refrigerate for several hours before serving.

AHEAD-OF-TIME NOTES

The cheesecake can be made a day in advance.

RUSTIC APPLE TART

Since the apples are not precooked before they are baked in this tart make sure you use a soft
or juicy variety of apple, such as Golden Delicious, Gala, or Sierra Beauty. This tart is good for breakfast,
as it is light, flaky, and not too sweet, but it's also good after a big meal.
Serve with Caramel Crème Fraîche (page 236) or the Apple Cider Ice (page 150).

SERVES 6

12 ounces Puff Pastry (see page 234)

1 egg, lightly beaten

2 apples, peeled, cored,
  and sliced ⅛ inch thick

1 tablespoon freshly squeezed lemon juice

2 tablespoons granulated sugar

1 tablespoon apple jelly, warmed

On a lightly floured work surface, roll the puff pastry in a 7- by 19-inch rectangle. Refrigerate the rolled puff pastry until firm, about 30 minutes.

Cutting off one end and one long side, trim the puff pastry into a 6- by 18-inch rectangle. Cut the scraps into ½ inch wide strips to use for the border of the tart. Brush the outside ½-inch edges of the rectangle with the beaten egg. Lay the puff pastry strips down each side and along each end over the egg wash. With a fork pierce small holes all over the bottom of the tart. To decorate the tart, press the edges of the tart with the blunt edge of a knife. Place the puff pastry on a baking sheet.

In a medium bowl combine the apples, lemon juice, and sugar. Arrange the apples, slightly overlapping, inside the tart. Refrigerate for 30 minutes.

Preheat the oven to 375 degrees.

Brush the apple tart with the warmed apple jelly. Bake until golden brown, 30 to 35 minutes. Serve the tart warm.

AHEAD-OF-TIME NOTES

The tart is best eaten the day it is made. It can be reheated. Store at room temperature.

ZINFANDEL PEARS WRAPPED IN PUFF PASTRY

A fellow pastry chef, Hollyce Snyder, devised this recipe for wrapping poached pears in strips of puff pastry. We like to call it pears in bondage! Serve with crème fraîche on the side.

SERVES 6

Pears

3 cups zinfandel wine

3¼ cups granulated sugar

2½ cups water

2 whole cloves

¼ teaspoon salt

1 vanilla bean, cut in half,
   with the insides scraped out

2 cups freshly squeezed orange juice

1 cinnamon stick

6 peppercorns

6 firm, ripe, tall and slender pears

PEARS

In a medium saucepan combine the zinfandel, sugar, water, cloves, salt, vanilla bean, orange juice, cinnamon stick, and peppercorns. Cook the mixture over medium heat until the sugar dissolves.

Peel the pears. From the bottom of each pear, core with a melon baller or small spoon. Work carefully so the pears do not break. Place them in the zinfandel mixture. Cover the pears with a dish towel. Poach over medium heat until a knife easily pierces the pear flesh, about 20 minutes. Remove the pears from the liquid and refrigerate until cool.

Reduce the pear poaching liquid over high heat until it thickens into a light syrup. Strain and cool the syrup. Set aside.

Wrapping the Pears

1 pound Puff Pastry (page 234)
1 large egg, lightly beaten
1 tablespoon granulated sugar

WRAPPING THE PEARS

On a lightly floured work surface, roll the puff pastry into an 8- by 14-inch rectangle. Using a fluted pastry wheel, cut the puff pastry lengthwise into ⅜- by 14-inch strips. Refrigerate until firm but not hard, about 30 minutes.

Preheat the oven to 375 degrees.

Place the end of a strip of puff pastry strip underneath one of the pears. Starting at the bottom, wrap the pear with this and additional strips. (Depending on the size of each pear, you may have to connect pieces of puff pastry strips together with beaten egg to wrap an entire pear.) Press the end of each strip against the top of the pear. Wrap the other pears in the same manner.

Brush the puff pastry with the beaten egg, being careful not to get egg on the pears. Sprinkle the puff pastry with the sugar. Bake the pears until the puff pastry is golden brown, about 25 to 30 minutes. As the pears bake, the puff pastry will shrink slightly, exposing the pears. Let the pears cool to room temperature.

Drizzle some of the reserved poaching syrup over the pears and serve.

AHEAD-OF-TIME NOTES

The pears can be poached a day in advance. The puff pastry strips can be rolled several days in advance and frozen. Refrigerate for at least an hour so that they become bendable before wrapping the pears. Wrap and bake the pears the day you plan to serve them.

MORNING APPLE CAKE

I like to call this morning apple cake because if it's the first thing you put in your mouth
in the morning (except for a good cup of coffee) it's bound to be a good day! After dinner serve this
with Caramel Crème Fraîche (page 236).

5 apples

1⅔ cups all-purpose flour

⅔ cup whole wheat flour

Pinch of ground cloves

1 teaspoon ground cinnamon

Pinch of ground mace

1 teaspoon baking soda

½ teaspoon salt

½ pound (2 sticks) unsalted butter, softened

1⅔ cups granulated sugar

2 large eggs

1 teaspoon vanilla extract

1 cup (4 ounces) walnuts, toasted and chopped

Equipment

A 9-inch bundt pan, buttered and floured

Preheat the oven to 325 degrees.

Peel, core and coarsely grate the apples. Set aside.

Sift together the all-purpose and whole wheat flours, cloves, cinnamon, mace, baking soda, and salt. Set aside.

In the bowl of an electric mixer, combine the butter and sugar. Using the paddle attachment, beat the mixture on medium speed until light. Add the eggs and vanilla extract and mix well. Decrease to low speed and add the reserved dry ingredients. Stir in the walnuts and grated apples.

Put the batter into the prepared bundt pan and bake until a skewer inserted in the middle comes out clean, about 1 hour. Let cool in the pan and then unmold it.

AHEAD-OF-TIME NOTES

The cake can be made a day in advance. Store wrapped in plastic wrap at room temperature.

AUTUMN HARVEST TART

I make this tart at Thanksgiving to be served alongside pumpkin pie. The dried fruit turns a rich dark brown color when baked, so it resembles a mincemeat tart, or really a "vegetarian mincemeat" tart! Serve with crème fraîche or whipped cream.

SERVES 6 TO 8

Streusel Topping

2 tablespoons (¼ stick) cold unsalted butter

¼ cup granulated sugar

¼ cup firmly packed dark brown sugar

½ cup all-purpose flour

⅛ teaspoon ground cinnamon

Fruit Filling

1 apple

1 small orange

½ lemon

½ cup chopped dried apricots

½ cup dried currants

½ cup golden raisins

½ cup brandy

¼ cup granulated sugar

¼ cup water

1 prebaked 9½-inch tart shell (page 226)

STREUSEL TOPPING

In a food processor, combine the butter, granulated and dark brown sugars, flour, and cinnamon. Using quick on-off turns, process the mixture until the butter is the size of small peas. Refrigerate until cold.

FRUIT FILLING

Peel, core, and chop the apple into ¼-inch pieces. Halve the orange and lemon and remove the ends and seeds. Chop the pulp and skin into ¼-inch pieces.

In a medium saucepan combine the chopped apple, orange, and lemon with the apricots, currants, golden raisins, brandy, sugar, and water. Cook over medium heat, stirring frequently, until the fruit is soft and the liquid is absorbed, about 15 minutes. Cool to room temperature.

Preheat the oven to 350 degrees.

Spread the fruit in the prebaked tart shell. Sprinkle the reserved streusel over the fruit. Bake until the streusel is browned, 30 to 35 minutes. Serve the tart warm or at room temperature.

AHEAD-OF-TIME NOTES

The streusel and the fruit filling can be made a day in advance and refrigerated. The tart should be assembled, baked, and eaten on the same day.

PEAR RIESLING TRIFLE

Puréeing the pears concentrates the pear flavor and produces a lovely purée in which to soak the genoise.

SERVES 8 TO 10

Pears

8 ripe firm pears

1½ cups granulated sugar

¼ cup Riesling wine

Pinch of salt

2 tablespoons freshly squeezed lemon juice

Riesling Sabayon

8 large egg yolks

½ cup granulated sugar

¾ cup Riesling wine

Pinch of salt

1¼ cups heavy whipping cream

For Assembly

1 recipe Vanilla Genoise (page 237)

Equipment

A 2½-quart bowl, preferably glass

PEARS

Peel, core and slice the pears ½ inch thick. Combine the pears in a large sauté pan with the sugar, Riesling, salt, and lemon juice. Cook over medium-high heat until the juices start to evaporate, 10 to 15 minutes. In a food processor, roughly purée the pears. Set aside to cool.

RIESLING SABAYON

Fill a medium saucepan ⅓ full of water. Bring the water to a low boil.

Fill a medium bowl with ice water. Set aside.

In a stainless steel bowl, whisk together the egg yolks, sugar, Riesling, and salt. Set the bowl into the pot of water, making sure that the water doesn't touch the bottom of the bowl. Cook, whisking constantly, until thick, about 3 minutes. Set the bowl in the bowl of ice water. Whisk until cool.

In a separate bowl, whisk the cream until soft peaks form. Fold it into the Riesling mixture. Refrigerate until you are ready to assemble the trifle.

ASSEMBLY

Cut the genoise in half horizontally with a knife.

Pour ⅓ cup of the sabayon in the 2½-quart glass bowl. Cut and fit pieces of the genoise over the sabayon in a single layer. Cover with ⅔ cup of the reserved pureé, then 1 cup of sabayon. Continue layering in the same manner, ending with sabayon.

Refrigerate for at least 6 hours before serving.

AHEAD-OF-TIME NOTES

The trifle can be made 1 to 2 days ahead.

PUMPKIN SOUFFLÉ WITH APPLE CARAMEL SAUCE

If sugar pumpkins are available, make your own pumpkin purée for this soufflé (page 233). If not, substitute canned pumpkin; just make sure that it does not have any added spices.

SERVES 6

1 cup Pumpkin Purée (page 233)

½ cup firmly packed dark brown sugar

⅛ teaspoon ground cloves

½ teaspoon ground cinnamon

⅛ teaspoon grated nutmeg

⅛ teaspoon ground ginger

Pinch of salt

12 large egg whites

½ cup granulated sugar

2 cups Apple Caramel Sauce (page 229)

Equipment

A 2-quart ovenproof soufflé dish, buttered and sugared

Preheat the oven to 375 degrees.

In a medium-sized bowl combine the pumpkin purée, brown sugar, cloves, cinnamon, nutmeg, ginger, and salt. Set aside.

Put the egg whites in the bowl of an electric mixer. Using the whip attachment on medium speed, whip until frothy. Increase to high speed and slowly add the granulated sugar in a steady stream. Whip until soft peaks form.

Fold the egg whites into the reserved pumpkin mixture. Gently spread the pumpkin mixture in the soufflé dish. Bake until firm around the edges and top, 25 to 30 minutes.

Serve the soufflé immediately with the sauce on the side.

AHEAD-OF-TIME NOTES

The pumpkin soufflé cannot be made in advance. The purée mixture can be made a day ahead.

CHESTNUT CREAM WITH PEARS

If you prefer, this light and creamy dessert can be made in individual portions instead of in a terrine.

SERVES 6

Chestnut Cream

1½ teaspoons powdered gelatin

3 tablespoons water

¾ cup plus 1½ teaspoons granulated sugar

¾ cup heavy whipping cream

1¼ cups sour cream

1 cup crème fraîche

¼ cup plus 2 tablespoons unsweetened
   chestnut purée

¼ teaspoon vanilla extract

Pinch of salt

Pears

6 ripe pears

⅓ cup granulated sugar

1 tablespoon freshly squeezed lemon juice

Pinch of salt

1 tablespoon unsalted butter

Equipment

A 9- by 5- by 3-inch terrine pan,
   lined with plastic wrap

CHESTNUT CREAM

In a small saucepan, mix together the gelatin and the water. Set aside for 10 minutes to soften.

Fill a medium saucepan ⅓ full of water. Bring the water to a boil.

In a stainless steel mixing bowl, whisk together the sugar, cream, sour cream, and crème fraîche. Set the bowl into the pot of boiling water, making sure that the water doesn't touch the bottom of the bowl. Cook the mixture, stirring occasionally, until hot. Remove the bowl from the heat.

Dissolve the gelatin mixture over low heat.

Whisk the chestnut purée, vanilla, and salt into the sour cream mixture. Add the dissolved gelatin. Pour the chestnut cream into the terrine pan. Refrigerate until set, several hours to overnight.

Unmold and refrigerate until ready to serve.

PEARS

Peel, core, and slice the pears ⅜ inch thick. In a large sauté pan, combine the pears, sugar, lemon juice, and salt. Cook over medium–high heat until the pears are cooked through but still retain their shape, 5 to 10 minutes. Strain the liquid from the pears. Return the liquid to the pan and reduce over high heat until lightly syrupy. Stir in the butter.

Place a slice of the chestnut cream on each plate. Spoon some of the pears over one end. Drizzle some pear syrup on top. Serve immediately.

AHEAD-OF-TIME NOTES

The chestnut cream can be made a day in advance. Cook the pears the day you serve the dessert.

CHESTNUT CRÊPES
WITH ORANGE HONEY ICE CREAM

This easy, elegant dessert is great for the holidays. Chestnut flour can be found in gourmet food stores.

SERVES 6

Chestnut Crêpes

½ cup milk

½ cup water

2 large eggs

¼ teaspoon vanilla extract

½ teaspoon finely chopped orange zest

½ cup chestnut flour

½ cup all-purpose flour

¼ cup granulated sugar

⅛ teaspoon salt

1 tablespoon unsalted butter, melted

Finishing the Dessert

1 cup freshly squeezed orange juice

1 tablespoon freshly squeezed lemon juice

⅓ cup Sugar Syrup (page 239)

Pinch of salt

6 tablespoons (¾ stick) unsalted butter

6 scoops Orange Honey Ice Cream
 (page 242)

CHESTNUT CRÊPES

In a food processor combine the milk, water, eggs, and vanilla extract. Process briefly to mix. Add the grated orange zest, chestnut and all-purpose flours, sugar, salt, and melted butter. Process for 1 minute. Refrigerate 1 hour to overnight.

Heat a 7-inch nonstick pan over medium high heat. Pour 1½ tablespoons of the crêpe batter in the pan and quickly rotate the pan, spreading a thin layer of batter over the bottom. Cook the crêpe for 2 minutes. Loosen the edge with a knife and turn the crêpe over. Cook for another 30 seconds. Place the crêpe on a plate. Continue to make crêpes in this manner until you have 18 crêpes. The cooked crêpes can be stacked slightly overlapping.

FINISHING

In a large sauté pan combine the orange juice, lemon juice, sugar syrup, and salt. Over medium-high heat bring the liquid to a boil. Place a crêpe in the pan and cover it with the juice. Fold the crêpe into quarters and move it to one side of the pan. Continue to add and fold the crêpes one at a time until all have been heated. Place 3 crêpes on each plate. Add the butter to the sauce and cook until the sauce starts to thicken, 2 to 3 minutes.

Place a scoop of orange honey ice cream in the middle of the crêpes and spoon the sauce around them. Serve immediately.

AHEAD-OF-TIME NOTES

The crêpes can be made ahead and refrigerated or frozen. The sauce should be made at the last minute.

FIGS WITH LEMON ALMOND GOAT CHEESE

Figs pair nicely with almost all cheeses. This recipe could also be made with Gorgonzola.

SERVES 6

18 ripe figs
¼ cup (1 ounce) whole almonds, toasted
6½ ounces goat cheese
1 tablespoon granulated sugar
1 teaspoon grated lemon zest
6 tablespoons heavy whipping cream

Preheat the broiler.

With a sharp knife cut into the figs from the top so that they open up but remain in one piece. Place them in a single layer in an ovenproof baking dish. Set aside.

Coarsely chop the almonds. In a small mixing bowl, combine the almonds, goat cheese, sugar, grated lemon zest, and cream. Mix until smooth. Fill the center of each fig with about 1 tablespoon of the goat cheese mixture.

Broil the figs until the cheese has melted and is bubbling, about 5 minutes. Serve immediately.

AHEAD-OF-TIME NOTES

The goat cheese can be prepared several hours in advance, but wait until the last minute to add the almonds so that they won't get soggy.

BAKED APPLES
WITH CARAMEL RUM RAISIN SAUCE

The addition of caramel rum raisin sauce makes these baked apples extra special. If you wish, you can fill the baked apples with vanilla ice cream instead of the crème fraîche.

SERVES 6

4 tablespoons (½ stick) unsalted butter, softened

¼ cup granulated sugar

2 teaspoons ground cinnamon

¼ teaspoon salt

¼ cup pure maple syrup

6 firm juicy apples

¾ cup crème fraîche

3 cups Caramel Rum Raisin Sauce (page 228)

Preheat the oven to 325 degrees.

In a small bowl, mix together the butter, sugar, cinnamon, salt, and maple syrup. Set aside.

Core the apples and put them in a baking dish in a single layer.

Fill the insides of the cored apples with the reserved butter mixture.

Place the apples in a baking pan and cover with foil. Bake until the apples are soft but still hold their shape, about 1 hour.

Place an apple on each of 6 plates. Spoon 2 tablespoons of the crème fraîche in each of the apples and pour some of the caramel rum raisin sauce around the base of each plate and over each apple. Serve extra sauce on the side.

AHEAD-OF-TIME NOTES

The apples can be baked ahead and reheated.

APPLE BRAID

This is probably more appropriate for breakfast than after dinner, but I feel great pastries mark the beginning of a great day. I have taken a typical cinnamon roll dough and filled it with apples, spices, and walnuts. Why start a day with a bagel when you can have a fresh, hot-from-the-oven slice of apple braid?

SERVES 8 TO 10

Filling

2 large apples

¼ cup firmly packed dark brown sugar

8 tablespoons (1 stick) unsalted butter, softened

2 teaspoons ground cinnamon

⅛ teaspoon ground cloves

¼ teaspoon grated nutmeg

Pinch of salt

½ cup (2 ounces) walnuts, toasted and coarsely chopped

Dough

1 tablespoon dry yeast

3 tablespoons warm milk

3 large eggs

2 tablespoons granulated sugar

2¾ cups all-purpose flour

½ teaspoon salt

12 tablespoons (1½ sticks) unsalted butter, softened

FILLING

Peel and core the apples. Chop into ⅛-inch pieces.

In a bowl of an electric mixer combine the brown sugar, butter, cinnamon, cloves, nutmeg, and salt. Using the paddle attachment, beat the mixture on medium speed until well combined. Reduce to low speed and mix in the walnuts and apples. Set aside.

DOUGH

In a clean bowl of an electric mixer combine the yeast and the warm milk. Proof for 10 minutes. Using the paddle attachment, on medium speed, add the eggs and mix until combined. Decrease to low speed and add the sugar, flour and salt, again mixing until combined. Increase to medium speed, add the butter, and mix until smooth. Place the dough in a buttered bowl, cover, and let proof until doubled, about 2 hours.

On a lightly floured work surface, roll the dough into a 12- by 15-inch rectangle. Spread the reserved filling evenly over the dough.

From a long end, roll the dough into a cylinder as you would a jelly roll. Cut the roll in half. Roll each half into a 16-inch log. Weave the two logs together by alternately crisscrossing them over each other. Press the logs together at both ends. Let the braid proof 1 hour.

Preheat the oven to 350 degrees.

Bake until golden brown, about 30 to 35 minutes.

Glaze

1 tablespoon sour cream

1 tablespoon freshly squeezed orange juice

1 teaspoon vanilla extract

1½ teaspoons finely chopped orange zest

1 cup confectioners' sugar

GLAZE

In a large bowl combine the sour cream, orange juice, vanilla extract, and orange zest. Add the confectioners' sugar and mix until smooth. Drizzle the glaze over the top of the warm apple braid.

AHEAD-OF-TIME NOTES

The apple braid can be assembled a day in advance. Refrigerate overnight and then let rest at room temperature for 30 minutes to 1 hour before baking. It is best eaten the day it is baked.

PEAR CHAUSSON

Puff pastry filled with fruit and served warm from the oven is one of the most perfect desserts in existence.
It is important to precook the pears or the puff pastry will get soggy.

SERVES 8

1 pound 6 ounces Puff Pastry (page 234)
6 ripe pears
½ cup plus 1 tablespoon granulated sugar
1 large egg, lightly beaten

Preheat the oven to 450 degrees.

Peel, halve, and core the pears. In a medium mixing bowl, coat the pears with ½ cup of the sugar. Place the pears on a baking sheet. Bake them until the pear juices begin to caramelize, about 25 minutes. Let cool to room temperature. Turn off the oven.

On a lightly floured work surface, divide the puff pastry in half. Refrigerate one of the pieces. Roll the remaining piece into a 10-inch square. Place a 10-inch round plate on top of the square and trim the puff pastry into a circle to make the bottom of the chausson. Refrigerate the 10-inch circle on a baking sheet.

Roll the second piece of puff pastry into a 12-inch square. Place a 12-inch round plate on top of the 12-inch square and trim the puff pastry into a circle, to make the top of the chausson. Refrigerate.

Place the pears on the 10-inch circle of puff pastry, leaving a 1-inch edge around the outside of the puff pastry. Brush some of the beaten egg around the edge. Place the 12-inch piece of puff pastry over the pears. Press the two pieces of puff pastry together, using the beaten egg to "glue" them together. Tuck the edge of the puff pastry under itself and decorate the edge with a fork.

Refrigerate for at least 30 minutes before baking.

Preheat the oven to 375 degrees.

Brush the chausson with the remaining beaten egg and sprinkle the top with the remaining 1 tablespoon sugar. Cut 5 small slits in the center of the top. Bake until it begins to brown, 10 to 15 minutes. Decrease the oven temperature to 350 degrees and bake until golden brown all over, about 15 minutes more.

Slice the chausson and serve warm.

AHEAD-OF-TIME NOTES

The puff pastry can be rolled a day in advance. The chausson can be assembled several hours before it is going to be baked. Refrigerate it and place it in the preheated oven directly from the refrigerator. The chausson is at its best if it is served warm from the oven.

HONEY MARSALA BAKED FIGS WITH FRESH GINGER SABAYON

In California, Black Mission figs have a short season in July and then they disappear for about a month, reappearing in the late summer for their grand finale.

SERVES 6

Figs

½ cup marsala

⅔ cup honey

1 teaspoon vanilla extract

18 ripe Black Mission figs

Ginger Sabayon

8 large egg yolks

½ cup freshly squeezed orange juice

¼ cup granulated sugar

1 tablespoon freshly grated fresh ginger

1½ cups heavy whipping cream

FIGS

In a mixing bowl whisk together the marsala, honey, and vanilla. Set aside ¼ cup of the mixture. Mix the figs into the remaining mixture. Let marinate for at least 15 minutes and up to several hours.

GINGER SABAYON

Fill a medium saucepan ⅓ full of water. Bring the water to a low boil.

Fill a medium bowl ⅓ full of ice water. Set aside.

In a medium stainless steel bowl, whisk together the egg yolks, orange juice, the ¼ cup marsala mixture, sugar, and grated ginger. Set the bowl into the pot of boiling water, making sure that the water doesn't touch the bottom of the bowl. Cook the sabayon, whisking constantly, until thick. Place the bowl in the bowl of ice water. Whisk until cool.

In a separate bowl, whisk the cream until soft peaks form. Fold in the ginger mixture. Refrigerate.

BAKING THE FIGS

Preheat the oven to 350 degrees.

Place the figs in a single layer in a baking dish. Pour the marsala liquid over them. Cover with aluminum foil. Bake for 10 minutes, turn the figs over and bake 10 minutes more until they are plump and soft.

Serve 3 figs per person, with a dollop of sabayon.

AHEAD-OF-TIME NOTES

The sabayon and the honey marsala mixture can be made ahead. Bake the figs just before serving them.

SWEET POTATO PUMPKIN TART
WITH SUGAR AND SPICE PUMPKIN SEEDS

I admit it—I have never been a big fan of pumpkin pie. Adding sweet potato to the mixture, plus the additional garnish of sugar and spice pumpkin seeds, makes it a dessert that even I look forward to. Serve with whipped cream.

SERVES 6

2 large eggs

⅓ cup firmly packed dark brown sugar

⅓ cup dark corn syrup

¾ cup heavy whipping cream

½ cup Pumpkin Purée (page 233)

½ cup Sweet Potato Purée (page 233)

2 teaspoons dark rum

¼ teaspoon salt

¼ teaspoon ground cinnamon

¼ teaspoon ground ginger

A prebaked 9½-inch tart shell (page 226)

2¼ cups Sugar and Spice Pumpkin Seeds (page 199)

Preheat the oven to 325 degrees.

In a medium bowl, combine the eggs, brown sugar, and corn syrup. Whisk until smooth. Whisk in the cream, pumpkin and sweet potato purées, rum, salt, cinnamon, and ginger. Pour the mixture into the prebaked tart shell.

Bake until set, about 25 to 30 minutes. Cool to room temperature. Sprinkle the sugar and spice pumpkin seeds on the tart and serve extra seeds in a bowl on the side.

AHEAD-OF-TIME NOTES

The tart is best served the day it is made. You can make the tart filling a day in advance, however, and refrigerate it.

HAZELNUT PEAR TART

Adding hazelnuts to the dough in this recipe gives the crust added flavor.

SERVES 8

Hazelnut Pastry Dough

¼ cup (1 ounce) hazelnuts,
  toasted and skinned

1½ tablespoons granulated sugar

2 cups all-purpose flour

⅛ teaspoon salt

½ pound (2 sticks) cold unsalted butter

2 tablespoons ice water

Pear Filling

1 large egg

2 large egg yolks

6 tablespoons granulated sugar

¾ cup heavy whipping cream

6 tablespoons crème fraîche

¼ teaspoon ground cardamom

Pinch of salt

3 ripe firm pears

A 9½-inch tart shell (page 226)

HAZELNUT PASTRY DOUGH

In a food processor, finely grind the hazelnuts and the sugar.

In a medium bowl, combine the hazelnut mixture, flour, and salt. Add the butter and mix with a pastry blender until the butter is the size of small peas. Add the water. Mix until the dough comes together. Form the dough into a ball. Chill for 30 minutes.

On a lightly floured work surface, roll the dough ¼ inch thick. Line the tart shell with the dough. Refrigerate for 30 minutes.

Preheat the oven to 350 degrees. Line the tart shell with parchment paper and fill with pie weights. Bake until the edges are golden, about 20 minutes. Remove the parchment paper and weights. Continue to bake until golden all over, about 10 minutes.

PEAR FILLING

Decrease the oven temperature to 325 degrees.

In a bowl, whisk together the egg, yolks, and sugar. Add the cream, crème fraîche, cardamom, and salt.

Peel, core, and slice the pears ⅛ inch thick. Arrange the pears in a circular pattern in the prebaked tart shell. Pour the custard over the pears until the tart is full. (There may be extra custard depending on the height of the sides of the tart shell.)

Bake until the custard is almost completely set, about 30 minutes.

Cool to room temperature before serving.

AHEAD-OF-TIME NOTES

The tart is best eaten the day it is baked. The dough can be made and put in the pan several days in advance.

CRANBERRY APPLE FALL PUDDING

Like its cousin, summer pudding, this dessert is made up of brioche that has been soaked in fruits and their juices. Here I have used cranberries and apples. Serve with Vanilla Crème Anglaise (page 232).

SERVES 8

4 cups cranberries

3 apples, peeled, cored, and coarsely chopped

2 cups apple juice

¾ cup granulated sugar

1 cinnamon stick

½ cup water

2 teaspoons freshly squeezed lemon juice

1½ pounds brioche or similar-textured bread

Equipment

1½-quart dish lined with plastic wrap

In a medium saucepan combine the cranberries, apple pieces, apple juice, sugar, and cinnamon stick. Cook over medium heat, stirring frequently until the fruit is soft, 10 to 15 minutes. Remove and discard the cinnamon stick.

In a food processor, purée the fruit mixture until smooth. Place the purée in a bowl and stir in the water and lemon juice.

Cut the crust from the brioche and slice ⅜ inch thick.

Spoon ¼ cup of the fruit purée into the bottom of the 1½-quart dish. Dip a slice of the brioche into the fruit purée, making sure it is completely coated. Place the piece of brioche in the dish. Continue placing pieces of fruit-soaked brioche in the dish until there is a single layer. (Cut pieces of bread to make them fit.) Spoon ¼ cup of fruit purée over the bread and again place a single layer of fruit-soaked bread on top. Continue with this layering process until the container is full.

Cover the pudding with plastic wrap and invert a plate on top. Be sure that the plate fits snugly inside the container. Place the pudding on a baking pan. Put a 2 to 3 pound weight on top of the pudding to press the layers together. Refrigerate overnight.

Remove the weight and plastic wrap. Invert the pudding and remove the dish and plastic wrap.

Serve the pudding. If there is extra fruit purée, serve it on the side.

AHEAD-OF-TIME NOTES

The pudding can be made a couple of days in advance. Refrigerate until ready to serve.

ÉCLAIRS WITH PEAR PASTRY CREAM

Éclairs are a classic dessert whose popularity has never waned.
Here, I have added pears to the pastry cream, making a great dessert even better.

I DOZEN 4-INCH ÉCLAIRS

Éclairs

¾ cup water

Pinch of salt

3 tablespoons unsalted butter

¼ teaspoon granulated sugar

¾ cup all-purpose flour

3 large eggs

Pear Pastry Cream

3 ripe pears

⅓ cup plus 2 tablespoons granulated sugar

1 teaspoon freshly squeezed lemon juice

6 large egg yolks

Pinch of salt

2 tablespoons cornstarch

1⅔ cups milk

1 piece of vanilla bean, 3 inches long

1 tablespoon unsalted butter

Equipment

A pastry bag with ½- and ¼-inch tips

ÉCLAIRS

Preheat the oven to 400 degrees.

Combine the water, salt, butter, and sugar in a heavy-bottomed saucepan. Bring to a boil over medium heat. When the mixture comes to a boil, remove the saucepan from the heat and stir in the flour, mixing well. Return the saucepan to the heat and cook, stirring constantly, until the dough comes cleanly away from the sides of the pot, about 1 minute.

Place the mixture in the bowl of an electric mixer and let it cool for 2 to 3 minutes. With the paddle attachment, start mixing the dough on medium speed. Add the eggs one at a time, beating well after each addition.

Place the ½-inch pastry tip in the pastry bag. Fill the pastry bag with the éclair batter. Pipe out 18 éclairs, each about 3½ inches long and ⅝ inch wide, onto a parchment-lined baking sheet.

Bake the éclairs for 15 minutes. Decrease the oven temperature to 350 degrees and continue to bake until golden brown and firm to the touch, about 15 minutes.

PEAR PASTRY CREAM

Peel and core the pears. Slice them ¼ inch thick. In a large sauté pan combine the pears with 2 tablespoons of the sugar and the lemon juice. Cook until the pears are soft and their liquid begins to evaporate.

In a food processor finely purée the pears. Set aside.

Place the egg yolks, remaining $\frac{1}{3}$ cup sugar, and salt in a mixing bowl and whisk until well blended. Stir in the cornstarch.

In a heavy-bottomed saucepan combine the milk and vanilla bean. Scald the milk over medium high heat. Whisk it slowly into the egg mixture.

Put the milk mixture back in the saucepan. Cook over medium low heat, stirring constantly until thick, about 5 minutes. Discard the vanilla bean. Strain the pastry cream through a medium sieve into a bowl. Stir in the butter and the reserved pear purée.

Place plastic wrap directly on the surface of the pastry cream to prevent a skin from forming as it cools. Refrigerate the pastry cream until cold.

Poke a small hole in the bottom of each éclair. Fit the $\frac{1}{4}$-inch pastry tip in the pastry bag. Fill the pastry bag with the pear pastry cream. Pipe the pastry cream into the éclairs.

Chocolate Glaze

4 ounces bittersweet chocolate

2 tablespoons ($\frac{1}{4}$ stick) unsalted butter

CHOCOLATE GLAZE

Melt the bittersweet chocolate and butter in a double boiler over simmering water, making sure that the water does not touch the bottom of the pan holding the chocolate. Whisk until smooth.

Dip the top of each éclair in the chocolate glaze. Place the éclairs, chocolate side up, on a platter and refrigerate until the chocolate is set.

AHEAD-OF-TIME NOTES

Éclairs are best eaten the day they are assembled. The pastry cream can be made 1 to 2 days in advance. The éclairs can also be baked a day in advance. Store them in an airtight container at room temperature. (If the éclairs get soggy before you get a chance to fill them, recrisp them in a preheated 300-degree oven for 5 minutes. They will crisp more as they cool.)

APPLE CIDER ICE

This ice can be served by itself or as a garnish to almost any fall dessert. It takes a little time for all of the ingredients to steep and infuse, but the kitchen smells wonderful in the process!

10 cups unfiltered apple cider

Peel of 1 orange

2 cinnamon sticks

Large pinch grated nutmeg

6 whole cloves

½ cup Calvados or apple brandy

2½ cups Sugar Syrup (page 239)

4 cups sparkling cider

4 teaspoons apple cider vinegar

2 tablespoons freshly squeezed lemon juice

In a large heavy-bottomed saucepan, combine all of the ingredients. Heat over high heat just until the mixture begins to simmer. Decrease to medium-low heat and let the mixture steep and reduce (but do not let it boil) to 8 cups, about 1 hour. Refrigerate until cold.

Pour the reduced apple liquid in a shallow pan. Freeze the mixture, stirring every ½ hour, until hard, about 3 to 4 hours.

AHEAD-OF-TIME NOTES

The ice can be made a day in advance. Before serving, break it up with a fork to give it a nice feathery texture.

APRICOT ALMOND BARS

Apricots and almonds are a great fruit-nut combination. Neither is overpowering and each brings out the best in the other.

A 9- BY 13-INCH PAN

Crust

10 tablespoons (1¼ sticks) cold unsalted butter

5 tablespoons granulated sugar

2 tablespoons lightly beaten egg

2 cups all-purpose flour

Fruit Filling

⅔ cup granulated sugar

1½ tablespoons honey

1 teaspoon freshly squeezed lemon juice

2 tablespoons light corn syrup

¼ cup heavy whipping cream

¼ cup milk

1⅔ cups (5 ounces) sliced almonds

1 cup coarsely chopped dried apricots

1 cup dried sour cherries

Equipment

A 9- by 13-inch pan

CRUST

In the bowl of an electric mixer using the paddle attachment, mix together the butter and sugar on low speed until combined. Stir in the beaten egg. Add the flour and mix until completely incorporated. Refrigerate the dough until firm, about 1 hour.

Preheat the oven to 350 degrees.

On a lightly floured board, roll the dough into a 15- by 12-inch rectangle. Place the dough in the pan. It should cover the bottom of the pan and come ½ inch up the sides. Trim the dough if necessary. Place a piece of parchment paper over the dough. Cover with pie weights and bake the dough until the edges are golden brown, about 20 minutes. Remove the weights and the parchment paper. Continue baking the crust until golden brown all over. Set aside to cool, leaving the oven on.

FRUIT FILLING

In a medium heavy-bottomed saucepan, combine the sugar, honey, lemon juice, and corn syrup. Bring the mixture to a boil over medium-high heat and cook until it is syrupy, 1 to 2 minutes. Remove the saucepan from the heat and stir in the cream and milk. Add the almonds, apricots, and cherries. Spread the fruit mixture over the reserved crust. Bake until the nuts are light golden in color, about 15 minutes. Cut the bars while they are still warm.

AHEAD-OF-TIME NOTES

The bars will keep for several days, but are best eaten the day they are baked. Store in an airtight container at room temperature.

CITRUS AND TROPICAL FRUITS

♦♦♦

A few years ago those tropical fruits known to most people
were limited to oranges, lemons, pineapples, and bananas. Now, with the
influx of immigrants from the tropics and the increased interest in Asian
and Mexican cooking, fruits such as mango, Key lime,
blood orange, passion fruit, and papaya are recognized in most households.
Desserts that were traditionally made with America's
indigenous fruits take on a new life when made with these tropical fruits.

LEMON CARAMEL SORBET

There is just enough caramel in this recipe to take the pucker out of the lemon.
It is very refreshing on a hot summer day. As always, when making caramel, be sure to wear oven mitts.

2 QUARTS

2¾ cups granulated sugar

3½ cups water

2 cups freshly squeezed lemon juice

In a medium heavy-bottomed saucepan, mix together 2 cups of the sugar and ½ cup water. Cook over medium heat until the sugar dissolves. Increase to high heat and cook until the sugar is golden amber in color. (Do not stir after you increase the heat.) Remove the saucepan from the heat and let the bubbles subside for about 5 seconds. Slowly stir in the remaining 3 cups water, a couple of tablespoons at a time. When the caramel bubbles up as the water is added, stop stirring for a minute and let the bubbles subside. Be careful—the caramel is hot. When all the water is added, stir in the lemon juice and remaining ¾ cup sugar. Refrigerate until cold.

Freeze in an ice cream machine according to manufacturer's instructions.

AHEAD-OF-TIME NOTES

The sorbet should be eaten within a day of being made. Any longer and the sorbet starts to separate.

ORANGE GRAND MARNIER SOUFFLÉ WITH CHOCOLATE CARAMEL SAUCE

I couldn't decide whether to serve chocolate or caramel sauce with this so I created chocolate caramel sauce!

SERVES 6

1½ cups milk

Peel of 1 orange

3 large egg yolks

⅓ cup granulated sugar

½ cup all-purpose flour

⅛ teaspoon salt

⅓ cup Grand Marnier

1 cup egg whites (about 8 large egg whites)

½ teaspoon cream of tartar

1 tablespoon confectioners' sugar

2 cups Chocolate Caramel Sauce (page 230)

Equipment

A 2-quart ovenproof soufflé dish, buttered and sugared

In a medium heavy-bottomed saucepan, combine the milk and the orange peel. Scald the milk over medium-high heat. Remove the saucepan from the heat, cover it, and steep for 10 minutes.

In a medium bowl whisk the egg yolks and sugar. Whisk in the flour and salt.

Strain the orange milk, discarding the peel. Whisk into the egg mixture. Stir in the Grand Marnier.

Pour the orange mixture back into the saucepan. Cook over medium heat, whisking constantly until thick, 2 to 3 minutes. Transfer to a clean bowl and cover with plastic wrap directly on the surface. Refrigerate until cold.

Preheat the oven to 350 degrees.

Place the egg whites in the bowl of an electric mixer. With the whisk attachment, whip the egg whites on medium speed until frothy. Add the cream of tartar. Increase to high speed and whip until stiff. Fold the egg whites into the orange base in two additions, working quickly yet gently.

Spread the soufflé batter in the prepared dish. Gently tap the dish on the work surface to remove any air bubbles. Bake until golden brown and the edges and top feel set when gently touched, 30 to 35 minutes.

Dust the soufflé with the confectioners' sugar and serve immediately, with the sauce on the side.

AHEAD-OF-TIME NOTES

The Grand Marnier mixture can be made a day in advance. Refrigerate until you are ready to make the soufflé.

PINEAPPLE BANANA COMPOTE
WITH MANGO SAUCE

As good-quality tropical fruit is available in the winter, this is a perfect fix for when I am in the mood for one of my favorite dessert combinations—warm fruit over ice cream. For a complete tropical treat serve this with the Macadamia Nut Biscotti (page 204) or the Coconut Sesame Cookies (page 208).

SERVES 6

3 ripe, firm bananas

½ of a fresh pineapple

½ cup firmly packed dark brown sugar

¾ cup freshly squeezed orange juice

3 tablespoons freshly squeezed lime juice

3 tablespoons dark rum

6 tablespoons (¾ stick) unsalted butter, softened

6 scoops Vanilla Ice Cream (page 240)

2 cups Mango Sauce (page 238)

Slice the bananas in half lengthwise and then into 1½-inch pieces. Peel and trim the pineapple and cut into ½ inch pieces. There should be about 3 cups of pineapple pieces. Set aside.

Combine the brown sugar, orange juice, lime juice, and rum in a large sauté pan. Cook over medium-high heat until the juices begin to boil and the sugar dissolves. Add the butter and continue to cook until the butter melts and the sauce thickens a little. Add the bananas and cook until they are warmed through, about 2 minutes. Add the pineapple.

Place the vanilla ice cream in bowls. Spoon the fruit compote over the vanilla ice cream and top with some mango sauce. Serve immediately.

A H E A D - O F - T I M E   N O T E S

The compote should be prepared at the last minute.

TANGERINE ICE

This is my favorite of all citrus sorbets and ices. Tangerines have such a distinct flavor, much more than any type of orange. Try to get honey tangerines. Serve with Pistachio Tuiles (page 212).

2 QUARTS

1⅓ cups granulated sugar

2 cups water

6 cups freshly squeezed tangerine juice

¼ teaspoon salt

2 teaspoons freshly squeezed lemon juice

In a small saucepan, stir together the sugar and 1 cup water. Over high heat, boil the mixtuture until the sugar is completely dissolved, about 1 minute. Cool to room temperature.

In a medium bowl combine the sugar syrup, tangerine juice, remaining 1 cup water, salt, and lemon juice. Pour the mixture into a shallow pan.

Freeze until firm, 4 hours to overnight. As it freezes, stir the ice with a fork every half hour or so to prevent it from freezing into a solid block. If the ice is frozen solid, break it up before serving it. The ice should have a feathery and flaky texture.

AHEAD-OF-TIME NOTES

The ice should be served within two days.

FROZEN ORANGE ESPRESSO MOUSSE

Two mousses, orange and espresso, are layered together to form this frozen terrine.
When they are poured into the pan they create a random pattern, making each slice a little different.
It's one of my favorites. It's also good with raspberry purée instead of the hot fudge sauce.

SERVES 8

Orange Cream

5½ ounces white chocolate, finely chopped

1½ cups heavy whipping cream

¼ cup milk

Peel of 1 orange

8 large egg yolks

2 tablespoons granulated sugar

2 tablespoons sour cream

1½ teaspoons finely chopped orange zest

1 tablespoon Grand Marnier

Equipment

1 terrine pan 9½ by 3½ by 4 inches,
   lined with plastic wrap

ORANGE CREAM

Put the white chocolate in a medium bowl. Set aside.

In a medium saucepan combine ¾ cup of the cream, the milk, and the orange peel. Scald the mixture. Remove the pot from the heat and cover it. Let the orange peel infuse in the cream for 25 minutes. Strain the orange peel from the cream and discard the peel.

Again scald the orange cream and pour it over the reserved white chocolate. Whisk until smooth.

In the bowl of an electric mixer, whip the egg yolks and sugar with the whisk attachment on high speed until thick. Reduce to medium-low speed and add the orange cream.

Return the orange mixture to the saucepan. Cook, stirring continually with a rubber spatula and scraping the bottom of the saucepan, over medium-low heat until thick, about 5 minutes. Remove the bowl from the heat and, whisking continually, cool to room temperature.

In a small bowl, combine the remaining ¾ cup of heavy cream, the sour cream, orange zest, and Grand Marnier. Whisk until soft peaks form. Fold the cream into the cooled orange mixture. Refrigerate the orange cream.

Espresso Cream

5½ ounces white chocolate, finely chopped

1½ cups heavy whipping cream

¼ cup milk

¼ cup espresso grounds

8 large egg yolks

1 tablespoon granulated sugar

2 tablespoons sour cream

2 cups Hot Fudge Rum Sauce (page 231)

ESPRESSO CREAM

Repeat the above procedure for the espresso cream, substituting the espresso grounds for the orange peel.

ASSEMBLY

Spread the espresso cream in the terrine. Pour the orange cream on top of the espresso cream. When you add the orange cream it will sink partly into the espresso cream, creating an uneven pattern. Freeze the bombe for several hours until firm.

Unmold the bombe, peel off the plastic wrap, and slice the terrine with a hot dry knife. Serve with the hot fudge rum sauce.

AHEAD-OF-TIME NOTES

The orange espresso mousse, whichever way you serve it, can be made a day or two in advance.

BANANA CARDAMOM CAKE

This cake is good by itself for breakfast or at tea time; it is also wonderful with some
Vanilla Crème Anglaise (page 232) and a drizzle of chocolate sauce.

SERVES 8

2 very ripe medium bananas

4 large eggs, separated

2 teaspoons vanilla extract

⅓ cup sour cream

1½ cups cake flour

1½ cups all-purpose flour

2 teaspoons baking powder

½ teaspoon salt

2 teaspoons ground cardamom

12 tablespoons (1½ sticks) unsalted butter,
    softened

1 cup firmly packed dark brown sugar

6 tablespoons granulated sugar

Equipment

A 9-inch bundt pan, buttered and floured

Preheat the oven to 325 degrees.

In a medium mixing bowl, mash the bananas. Stir in the egg yolks, vanilla extract, and sour cream. Set aside.

Sift together the cake flour, all-purpose flour, baking powder, salt, and cardamom.

In the bowl of an electric mixer using the paddle attachment, cream together the butter and brown sugar on medium-high speed until light.

Reduce to low speed and add half the banana mixture. Mix until almost combined and then add half the dry ingredients. Add the remaining banana mixture and then the remaining dry ingredients. Do not overmix.

In a clean bowl of an electric mixer, whip the egg whites on medium speed until frothy. Increase to high speed and slowly add the granulated sugar. Whip until soft peaks form. Fold the egg whites into the banana batter.

Spread the batter in the prepared bundt pan. Bake until a skewer inserted in the middle comes out clean, about 55 to 60 minutes.

Cool the cake completely and then remove it from the pan.

AHEAD-OF-TIME NOTES

The cake can be made a day in advance. Store wrapped in plastic wrap at room temperature.

KEY LIME PIE

Having lived in southwest Florida I appreciate a good Key lime pie and am horrified by those who use regular limes and still call it a Key lime pie. This is how a Key lime pie should taste—simple and tart. I substituted gingersnaps for the graham crackers to give the crust a little zip. Floridians tell me that a true Key lime pie must have a whipped cream topping, never meringue. You can buy Key lime juice at most gourmet food stores.

A 9-INCH PIE

Ginger Crust

1½ cups finely ground Snappy Gingersnaps (page 213)

4 tablespoons (½ stick) unsalted butter, melted

Filling

4 eggs

1½ cups plus 2 tablespoons granulated sugar

¾ cup Key lime juice

1 teaspoon finely chopped lime zest

8 tablespoons (1 stick) unsalted butter

1 cup heavy whipping cream

Equipment

A 9-inch pie pan

GINGER CRUST

Preheat the oven to 300 degrees.

In a mixing bowl, stir together the gingersnap crumbs and melted butter. Press the crumbs in the bottom and up the sides of the pie pan.

Bake the crust for 15 minutes. Cool.

FILLING

Fill a medium saucepan ⅓ full of water. Bring the water to a boil.

In a medium stainless steel mixing bowl whisk together the eggs and 1½ cups of the sugar until smooth. Stir in the Key lime juice and lime zest.

Set the bowl into the pot of boiling water, making sure the water doesn't touch the bottom of the bowl. Cook the mixture, whisking occasionally until thick. Remove the bowl from the heat and whisk in the butter.

Pour the Key lime mixture into the prepared pie crust. Refrigerate until cold, about 1 hour.

In a medium bowl whip the cream with the remaining 2 tablespoons sugar until soft peaks form. Pipe or spread the whipped cream over the top of the pie. Refrigerate until ready to serve.

AHEAD-OF-TIME NOTES

The crust and filling can be made a day in advance. Put the filling in the pie on the day you plan to serve it. Whip the cream and put it on the pie within a few hours of serving.

ORANGE MARMALADE CAKE

Spreading marmalade between the layers of an orange-flavored cake gives it a real citrus punch—one that can stand up to the chocolate glaze.

SERVES 8 TO 10

Orange Cake

4 cups all-purpose flour

1¼ teaspoons baking powder

½ teaspoon salt

¾ cup freshly squeezed orange juice

1 tablespoon finely chopped lemon zest

3 tablespoons freshly squeezed lemon juice

½ cup water

8 ounces (1 stick) unsalted butter, softened

2¼ cups granulated sugar

5 large eggs

Chocolate Glaze

4 ounces bittersweet chocolate, finely chopped

5 tablespoons unsalted butter

2 teaspoons corn syrup

2 cups good-quality orange marmalade

Equipment

Three 9-inch cake pans, buttered and floured

ORANGE CAKE

Preheat the oven to 350 degrees.

Sift together the flour, baking powder, and salt.

In a small bowl stir together the orange juice, lemon zest, lemon juice, and water.

Combine the butter and sugar in the bowl of an electric mixer. Using the paddle attachment beat the mixture until light, 3 to 5 minutes. Add the eggs one at a time. Reduce to low speed and alternately add the reserved flour mixture and orange juice mixture. Divide the batter among the three pans.

Bake until a skewer inserted in the middle comes out clean, about 30 minutes. Let cool to room temperature and then unmold.

CHOCOLATE GLAZE

Melt the chocolate, butter, and corn syrup in a double boiler over simmering water, making sure that the water does not touch the bottom of the pan holding the chocolate. Whisk until smooth. Set aside for 10 minutes to thicken slightly.

FINISHING

Spread the marmalade on two of the cakes. Stack one on top of the other. Top with the third cake. Pour the chocolate glaze over the top of the cake, letting it drizzle down the sides. Smooth the glaze over the sides and top. Let set for 15 minutes. Decorate the top and sides with the tines of a fork.

AHEAD-OF-TIME NOTES

The cake can be made a day in advance. Store at room temperature.

MANGO RASPBERRY FOOLS

A fruit fool, as opposed to the human type, is something to seek.
Fruit purée folded into whipped cream is the simple definition of a fool, but the varieties and combinations
are endless. Serve with Macadamia Nut Brittle on the side (page 210).

SERVES 6 TO 8

Mango Fool

3 ripe mangoes

Pinch of salt

2 cups heavy whipping cream

⅓ cup granulated sugar

Raspberry Fool

1½ cups heavy whipping cream

¼ cup granulated sugar

1½ cups unsweetenened Raspberry Purée
   (page 238)

MANGO FOOL

Peel the mangoes and remove the mango pulp
from the seed. In a food processor, purée the pulp.
Strain the mango purée through a medium sieve.
Stir in the salt.

In a medium mixing bowl, whip the cream with
the sugar until soft peaks form. Fold the cream into
the mango purée.

RASPBERRY FOOL

In a medium mixing bowl, combine the cream and
the sugar. Whip until soft peaks form.

Fold the raspberry purée into the cream.

Alternately layer the mango and raspberry creams
in tall clear glasses. Refrigerate until ready to serve.

AHEAD-OF-TIME NOTES

The mango and raspberry fools can be made a day in
advance, but wait until the day you plan to serve them to
layer them in the glasses.

BLOOD ORANGE TART

Blood oranges are beautiful in this tart, as their juices provide such a vibrant red color. If you can't find blood oranges, substitute other oranges or tangerines; just make sure that they are a variety with thin skins.

3 blood oranges

1½ cups granulated sugar

6 tablespoons freshly squeezed lemon juice

5 tablespoons freshly squeezed lime juice

Large pinch of salt

3 large eggs, lightly beaten

3 tablespoons all-purpose flour

A prebaked 9½-inch tart shell (page 226)

Slice the oranges paper-thin. Discard the seeds. In a mixing bowl, combine the orange slices, sugar, lemon juice and lime juice. Let marinate for 2 hours.

Preheat the oven to 325 degrees.

In a food processor, coarsely chop the orange mixture into ⅛-inch pieces. Return the orange mixture to the mixing bowl and mix in the salt, eggs, and flour.

Pour the orange mixture into the prebaked tart shell. Bake the tart until almost completely set, about 30 minutes.

Cool to room temperature before serving.

AHEAD-OF-TIME NOTES

The tart is best eaten the day it is baked.

LEMON CURD CAKE

Unadorned lemon cakes may seem simple, but when tasted, one realizes they do not need embellishments.

SERVES 8 TO 10

4 large egg yolks

2 large eggs

2¾ cups granulated sugar

½ cup plus 3 tablespoons freshly squeezed lemon juice

2 cups sifted cake flour

½ teaspoon salt

1 tablespoon baking powder

4 tablespoons (½ stick) unsalted butter, softened

2 teaspoons finely chopped lemon zest

6 large egg whites

1 tablespoon confectioners' sugar

Equipment

A 9-inch round by 3-inch-high cake pan, buttered and floured

Fill a medium saucepan ⅓ full of water. Bring the water to a low boil.

In a medium stainless steel bowl whisk together the egg yolks, eggs, and ½ cup of the sugar. Stir in ½ cup of the lemon juice.

Set the bowl into the pot of boiling water, making sure the water doesn't touch the bottom of the bowl. Cook the mixture, stirring occasionally until thick, about 10 minutes. Strain the lemon curd. Place plastic wrap directly on the surface. Chill until cold.

Sift together the cake flour, ¾ cup of the sugar, the salt, and baking powder. Set aside.

In a large mixing bowl, mix together the lemon curd, butter, lemon zest, and remaining 3 table-spoons lemon juice. Mix until well combined. Stir in the dry ingredients.

Preheat the oven to 325 degrees.

In the bowl of an electric mixer using the whip attachment, whip the egg whites on medium speed until frothy. Increase to high speed and gradually add the remaining 1½ cups sugar. Whip until soft peaks form.

Fold the egg whites into the cake batter. Spread the cake batter in the cake pan.

Bake until a skewer inserted in the middle comes out clean, about 50 to 55 minutes. Cool and then unmold the cake.

To serve, dust the cake with confectioners' sugar.

AHEAD-OF-TIME NOTES

The cake can be made a day in advance. Store wrapped in plastic wrap at room temperature.

BITTER ORANGE CRÈME CARAMEL

Reducing the orange juice gives this dessert a slightly bitter edge.

SERVES 8

Bitter Orange Custard

2 ¼ cups freshly squeezed orange juice

6 large egg yolks

¾ cup granulated sugar

Large pinch of salt

3 cups heavy whipping cream

Caramel

¾ cup granulated sugar

¼ cup water

Equipment

Eight 4-ounce ramekins

A baking pan large enough to hold all the ramekins

BITTER ORANGE CUSTARD

In a small heavy-bottomed saucepan reduce the orange juice over medium heat to 1 cup.

In a medium mixing bowl whisk together the egg yolks, sugar, and salt. Stir in the reduced orange juice.

In a medium heavy-bottomed saucepan, scald the cream. Whisk it into the orange mixture. Strain through a medium sieve. Refrigerate until cold.

CARAMEL

In a small heavy-bottomed saucepan, mix together the sugar and water. Cook the sugar over medium heat until it dissolves. Increase to high heat and cook the sugar until it is golden amber in color. (Do not stir after you increase the heat.) Remove the caramel from the heat and pour a couple of teaspoons into a ramekin. Quickly swirl the ramekin, coating the bottom with caramel. Be careful—the caramel is very hot. Repeat for all 8 ramekins. Set them aside so that the caramel can harden.

Preheat the oven to 300 degrees.

Fill the ramekins with the bitter orange custard. Place them in the large baking pan. Place the baking pan on a rack in the middle of the oven. Carefully fill the baking pan with water so it comes halfway up the sides of the ramekins. Cover the pan with aluminum foil. Bake until almost completely set, 40 to 50 minutes. Remove the ramekins from the baking pan. Refrigerate until cold, at least 6 hours. To unmold, run a small knife around the inside edge of each ramekin and invert onto a plate.

AHEAD-OF-TIME NOTES

The custards can be baked a day before you plan to serve.

RAINBOW SHERBET

*This dessert was created in memory of the rainbow sherbet we had as kids.
I remember eating it when I was home with a sore throat or the flu. It always made me feel better.
Serve with Marmalade Window Cookies (page 215).*

SERVES 8

Lemon Sherbet

1 cup freshly squeezed lemon juice

1 cup heavy whipping cream

½ cup milk

6 tablespoons light corn syrup

Pinch of salt

1 teaspoon finely chopped lemon zest

½ cup water

1¼ cups granulated sugar

Orange Sherbet

1 cup freshly squeezed orange juice

1 cup heavy whipping cream

½ cup milk

6 tablespoons light corn syrup

Pinch of salt

1½ teaspoons finely chopped orange zest

½ cup water

6 tablespoons granulated sugar

Raspberry Sherbet

½ cup unsweetened Raspberry Purée
  (page 238)

1 cup heavy whipping cream

½ cup milk

6 tablespoons light corn syrup

Pinch of salt

1 teaspoon freshly squeezed lemon juice

½ cup granulated sugar

LEMON SHERBET

In a small heavy-bottomed saucepan, reduce the lemon juice over medium-high heat to ½ cup.

In a mixing bowl whisk the reduced lemon juice with all of the other ingredients.

Freeze in an ice cream machine according to manufacturer's instructions.

ORANGE SHERBET

Follow the instructions for the lemon sherbet, substituting the orange juice for the lemon juice and the orange zest for the lemon zest.

Freeze in an ice cream machine according to manufacturer's instructions.

RASPBERRY SHERBET

In a mixing bowl, whisk together the raspberry purée, cream, milk, corn syrup, salt, lemon juice, and sugar.

Freeze in an ice cream machine according to manufacturer's instructions.

TO SERVE

Serve one scoop of each sherbet in ice cream glasses or bowls, or let your guests serve themselves, giving each the option of taking more of his or her favorite.

AHEAD-OF-TIME NOTES

The sherbets can all be made a couple of days in advance.

BANANA NAPOLEON
WITH WARM CARAMEL WALNUT SAUCE

This is the best of all banana desserts. Nothing more needs to be said.

SERVES 6

1 pound Puff Pastry (page 234)

Caramel Walnut Sauce

1 cup (4 ounces) walnuts, toasted
6 tablespoons (¾ stick) unsalted butter
1 cup firmly packed dark brown sugar
½ cup granulated sugar
⅔ cup heavy whipping cream
2 teaspoons vanilla extract

PUFF PASTRY

On a lightly floured work surface divide the puff pastry into two pieces. Put one piece in the refrigerator. Roll out the remaining piece into a 12- by 9-inch rectangle. Be sure to keep the top and bottom of the puff pastry lightly floured so it will not stick to the table or the rolling pin. Keep the pastry in an even rectangular shape as you roll. (If the sides get wider than the middle, roll out the middle, putting pressure on one end of the pin only.) Brush off any excess flour. Pierce small holes all over the puff pastry with the tines of a fork. With a sharp knife, cut the pastry into 3- by 4-inch rectangles. Place the pastry rectangles in the freezer and roll out the other half of the pastry in the same manner. There should be 18 rectangles of puff pastry. Freeze them for at least 1 hour.

CARAMEL WALNUT SAUCE

Coarsely chop the walnuts and set aside.

In a heavy-bottomed saucepan, melt the butter over medium-low heat. Stir in the brown and granulated sugar. Cook until smooth, about 5 minutes. Stir in the cream and vanilla extract. Cook until the sugar has dissolved and the sauce has thickened slightly, about 5 minutes. Add the reserved walnuts.

Finishing the Dessert

6 *medium ripe bananas*

1 *tablespoon freshly squeezed lemon juice*

1 *tablespoon dark rum*

3 *cups Whipped Cream (page 225)*

FINISHING

Preheat the oven to 375 degrees.

Place the frozen puff pastry on baking sheets in a single layer. Place an inverted wire mesh rack or another baking sheet on top of the puff pastry. (This will prevent it from rising as it cooks.) Bake the puff pastry until golden brown, 10 to 15 minutes.

Slice the bananas on the diagonal ½ inch thick. Place the bananas in a mixing bowl and gently combine them with the lemon juice and rum.

Place one piece of puff pastry on each of 6 plates. Spoon the bananas on top of the puff pastry. Place a second piece of pastry on top of the bananas. Dollop some whipped cream on the second piece of pastry, and pour some caramel walnut sauce over the cream and on the plate. Top with a third piece of puff pastry. Serve immediately.

AHEAD-OF-TIME NOTES

The puff pastry can be rolled and frozen several days in advance. Bake the puff pastry within a few hours of eating it. The sauce can be made ahead and reheated. Wait until you have reheated the sauce to add the walnuts so that the walnuts do not get soggy. Slice the bananas just before serving.

COCONUT CREAM PIE
WITH MANGO AND BLACKBERRY SAUCES

Mango and blackberry sauces add both color and taste to this classic pie.

2 cups shredded sweetened coconut

8 large egg yolks

½ cup granulated sugar

⅛ teaspoon salt

3 tablespoons cornstarch

2½ cups milk

½ vanilla bean

2 tablespoons unsalted butter, softened

A 9-inch prebaked pie shell (page 226)

1½ cups crème fraîche

1½ cups Mango Sauce (page 238)

1½ cups sweetened Blackberry Purée (page 238)

Preheat the oven to 350 degrees.

Place the coconut in a single layer on a baking tray. Toast the coconut until golden brown, about 10 minutes. The edges will toast faster than the middle so stir the coconut every couple of minutes for even baking. Turn off the oven.

In a medium mixing bowl, whisk together the egg yolks, sugar, salt and cornstarch.

Put the milk and the vanilla bean in a heavy-bottomed saucepan. Scald the milk and slowly whisk it into the egg mixture. Stir in 1½ cups of the toasted coconut.

Put the coconut mixture back into the saucepan. Cook over medium heat, stirring constantly until thick, making sure to scrape the bottom of the pan, about 10 minutes. Remove the saucepan from the heat and whisk in the butter. Discard the vanilla bean. Put the mixture in a clean bowl and place plastic wrap directly on the surface. Refrigerate until cold.

Spread the coconut cream in the prebaked pie shell. Whip the crème fraîche until thick and spread it over the pie. Sprinkle the remaining ½ cup coconut over the top. Spoon some blackberry and mango sauces on opposite sides of each plate. Place a piece of pie on top. Serve immediately.

AHEAD-OF-TIME NOTES

The coconut filling can be made a day in advance. Assemble and serve the pie on the same day.

CAMPARI TANGERINE SORBET

The Campari gives the sorbet a slightly bitter taste that is then softened by the sweetness of the tangerine juice. A subtle yet intriguing combination. Serve this with Coconut Sesame Cookies (page 208).

½ cup Campari

4 cups freshly squeezed and strained tangerine juice

1¼ cups Sugar Syrup (page 239)

Large pinch of salt

1½ teaspoons freshly squeezed lemon juice

In a mixing bowl combine all of the ingredients.

Freeze in an ice cream machine according to manufacturer's instructions. Alternatively, place the mixture in a large shallow pan and place it in the freezer. Freeze the mixture, stirring every half hour until frozen.

AHEAD-OF-TIME NOTES

The sorbet can be made a day in advance.

TROPICAL COOLER

On a much appreciated vacation on Kauai with my husband, we concocted this recipe, coconut sherbet served with fresh pineapple. It tastes like a piña colada without the alcohol.

SERVES 8

13½ ounces unsweetened coconut milk

½ cup light corn syrup

¾ cup granulated sugar

2 cups milk

¼ teaspoon salt

1 medium pineapple

In a medium saucepan combine the coconut milk, corn syrup, sugar, milk, and salt. Cook the mixture over medium-low heat until the sugar has dissolved and the mixture is smooth.

Pour the mixture into a shallow pan and freeze until hard, stirring every 30 minutes.

Peel and core the pineapple. Cut the pineapple into 1-inch pieces.

Serve the coconut sherbet in bowls with the pineapple.

AHEAD-OF-TIME NOTES

The coconut sherbet can be made several days in advance. Prepare the pineapple just before serving.

PASSION FRUIT MERINGUE TARTLETS

If you can't find fresh passion fruit, passion fruit juice is available by mail from Sid Wainer and Son, Specialty Produce and Specialty Foods, (800) 423-8333. If using fresh passion fruit, cut the fruit in half, scoop out the insides and purée the pulp. You will need about 9 passion fruit to yield 1 cup of juice.

SERVES 6

Passion Fruit Curd

7 large egg yolks

2 large eggs

¼ cup granulated sugar

¾ cup passion fruit juice

6 prebaked 4-inch tartlet shells (page 226)

Meringue

6 large egg whites

1½ cups granulated sugar

Equipment

A pastry bag fitted with a large decorative tip

PASSION FRUIT CURD

Fill a medium saucepan ⅓ full of water. Bring the water to a low boil.

In a stainless steel bowl whisk together the egg yolks, eggs, and sugar. Stir in the passion fruit juice.

Set the bowl into the pot of water, making sure the water doesn't touch the bottom of the bowl. Cook the mixture, stirring frequently until thick, about 10 minutes. Strain the curd. Place plastic wrap directly on the surface and refrigerate until cold.

Fill the tartlet shells with the curd. Set aside.

MERINGUE

Preheat the oven to 450 degrees.

Fill a medium pot ⅓ full of water. Bring the water to a low boil.

In a bowl of an electric mixer, whisk together the egg whites and sugar. Place the bowl in the hot water and cook, whisking continually, until hot. Remove from the water and place the bowl on the electric mixer. Whip on medium speed until stiff.

Place the meringue in the pastry bag. Pipe it on top of the tartlets, completely covering the curd.

Bake the tartlets until the meringue is golden brown, about 5 to 10 minutes.

Serve the tartlets warm or at room temperature.

AHEAD-OF-TIME NOTES

The tartlets are best served within a couple of hours being baked. The curd can be made a day in advance.

BANANA TARTE TATIN

Traditionally made with apples, a Tarte Tatin is just as delicious with bananas.
Serve with either crème fraîche or Mango Sauce (page 238).

SERVES 6 TO 8

8 ounces *Puff Pastry (page 234)*

2 tablespoons *freshly squeezed lemon juice*

1 cup *granulated sugar*

2 tablespoons *unsalted butter,*
broken into small pieces

3 large *bananas*

Equipment

A 9-inch round nonstick pan

On a lightly floured work surface, roll the puff pastry into a 9½-inch circle. Freeze until firm.

Preheat the oven to 450 degrees.

Place the lemon juice, sugar, and butter in the bottom of the nonstick pan. Cut the bananas in half lengthwise and place them, cut side up, in the pan. Cover the bananas with the frozen puff pastry. (The puff pastry will shrink a little as it cooks so it needs to be bigger than the pan.)

Bake until the puff pastry is golden brown in color and the sauce around the bananas is caramelized, 20 to 30 minutes. (If the puff pastry turns brown before the sauce has caramelized, remove the pan from the oven and finish cooking the caramel on top of the stove over medium high heat.)

Carefully invert the tarte Tatin onto a large serving platter. Serve warm.

AHEAD-OF-TIME NOTES

Tarte Tatins are best served warm from the oven. The puff pastry can be made several days in advance. Store it wrapped in plastic wrap in the freezer.

BANANA FRITTERS WITH MAPLE SYRUP SAUCE

These fritters are like sautéed corn fritters, not the deep-fried kind, which can be heavy to eat and messy to make. They are perfect for dessert or a weekend brunch.

SERVES 6

4 or 5 large bananas

3 large eggs, separated

1 tablespoon granulated sugar

1 tablespoon all-purpose flour

¼ teaspoon salt

2 tablespooons unsalted butter

1½ cups crème fraîche

1½ cups Maple Syrup Sauce (page 239)

Cut the bananas into ½-inch pieces. There should be 3 cups of diced bananas. Set aside.

In a medium mixing bowl combine the egg yolks and sugar. Stir in the chopped bananas, flour, and salt.

In a small mixing bowl, whip the egg whites until stiff. Fold the egg whites into the banana mixture.

In a large sauté pan melt the butter over medium-high heat. Spoon about 2 tablespoons of the banana mixture into the pan to make a fritter. Place as many fritters in the pan as possible without letting them touch. Cook until the bottoms are golden brown, 3 to 5 minutes. Turn them over and cook the other side until golden brown. Continue this procedure until there are 18 fritters. If you need to make a second batch of fritters, keep the first batch warm by covering them with a towel while you cook the second batch.

Place 3 fritters on each of 6 plates. Spoon some crème fraîche in the middle of the fritters. Drizzle some of the maple syrup sauce over the fritters and serve immediately. Serve any extra crème fraîche and maple syrup sauce on the side.

AHEAD-OF-TIME NOTES

The fritters must be made just before serving.

ORANGE PECAN CREAM SANDWICH

Pecan meringues layered with chocolate ganache and orange cream make up this refined ice cream sandwich.

SERVES 6 TO 8

Pecan Meringues

¾ cup (3 ounces) pecans, toasted

¾ cup plus 2 tablespoons granulated sugar

½ cup confectioners' sugar

6 large egg whites

Equipment

A pastry bag fitted with a ¼-inch round tip

PECAN MERINGUES

Preheat the oven to 225 degrees.

Line two baking sheets with parchment paper. Trace four 8-inch circles onto the parchment paper.

In a food processor, finely grind the pecans with ¼ cup of the granulated sugar and all the confectioners' sugar. Set aside.

Put the egg whites in the bowl of an electric mixer. With the whisk attachment, whip on medium speed until frothy. Increase to high speed and slowly add 2 tablespoons of the sugar. Continue to whip until soft peaks form. Slowly add the remaining ½ cup sugar and continue whipping until stiff.

Gently fold the reserved pecan mixture into the egg whites.

Fill the pastry bag with the pecan meringue. Using the 8-inch circle as a template, pipe a solid coil of the meringue in a circular motion starting at the inside of the circle. Pipe out three more meringue circles like the first one.

Bake until the meringues are dry and easily peel off the parchment paper, 2 to 3 hours.

Ganache

½ cup heavy whipping cream

4 ounces bittersweet chocolate, finely chopped

GANACHE

In a small heavy-bottomed saucepan scald the cream. Remove the pot from the heat and add the chocolate. Whisk until smooth. Refrigerate the ganache until it is firm yet still spreadable, about 30 minutes.

Orange Cream

2 tablespoons granulated sugar

3 tablespoons freshly squeezed orange juice

1 cup heavy whipping cream

¾ cup mascarpone

Pinch of salt

1½ teaspoons Grand Marnier

Decoration

¼ teaspoon cocoa powder

1 teaspoon confectioners' sugar

ORANGE CREAM

In the bowl of an electric mixer combine the sugar, orange juice, cream, mascarpone, salt, and Grand Marnier. Using the whisk attachment, whip the orange cream until stiff.

ASSEMBLY

Spread half of the ganache gently over one of the pecan meringues. Spread the remaining ganache over a second meringue. Refrigerate the meringues until the ganache is set, about 15 minutes. Spread ⅓ of the orange cream over each of the chocolate-coated meringues and one of the remaining meringues. Stack these three meringues on top of each other, placing the meringue without the ganache in the middle. Top with the fourth meringue.

In a small bowl, combine the cocoa powder and confectioners' sugar. Dust the top of the sandwich with the cocoa sugar.

Freeze for several hours until firm. Two to three hours before you plan to serve the sandwich, transfer it to the refrigerator. This will let it defrost a little so it will not be too hard to eat.

Slice with a serrated knife, using a sawing motion.

AHEAD-OF-TIME NOTES

The sandwich can be made a couple of days in advance. Store in the freezer.

TANGERINE RICE PUDDING

*I use arborio rice when I make rice pudding. Traditionally used in risotto, arborio produces
a very creamy rice pudding. Add tangerine zest and it really comes alive. If desired, you can serve this
with a little sweetened Raspberry Purée (page 238).*

SERVES 8

6⅓ cups water

2 cups arborio rice

3 large egg yolks

2 large eggs

Pinch of salt

1¼ cups milk

1½ cups heavy whipping cream

¾ cup granulated sugar

1 tablespoon finely chopped tangerine zest

Grated nutmeg for garnish

Equipment

A 3-quart baking dish

A baking pan large enough to hold
the baking dish

Preheat the oven to 325 degrees.

In a large saucepan bring the water to a boil over medium-high heat. Add the arborio rice and boil, stirring frequently, for 15 minutes. Strain the rice, discarding the water. Rinse the rice and cool to room temperature. There should be 4 cups of cooked rice.

Place the cooked rice in the 3-quart baking dish. Set aside

In a medium mixing bowl lightly whisk together the egg yolks, eggs, and salt. Set aside.

In a medium saucepan combine the milk, ½ cup of the cream, sugar, and tangerine zest. Scald the cream mixture and whisk it into the beaten eggs. Stir the custard mixture into the rice.

Place the baking dish in the large baking pan. Fill the baking pan with water so that the water comes ⅓ up the sides of the baking dish. Cover the baking dish. Bake, stirring every 10 minutes, until the custard has thickened but is not completely set, 40 to 45 minutes. Be careful not to overcook the pudding. Remove the pudding from the oven. Stir in the remaining 1 cup cream.

Serve the rice pudding at once, with sprinklings of freshly grated nutmeg.

AHEAD-OF-TIME NOTES

The pudding is best served warm from the oven.

AUSTRALIAN HUMMINGBIRD CAKE

This recipe was given to me by Karen Gough, an Australian now residing in San Francisco. She served this cake at her café in Perth, Australia. Karen doesn't know how the cake got its name, but she does know that it was her most popular dessert.

SERVES 8 TO 10

Cake

2⅔ cups all-purpose flour

2¼ cups granulated sugar

1 teaspoon salt

1 teaspoon baking soda

1 teaspoon ground cinnamon

3 eggs, lightly beaten

¾ pound (3 sticks) unsalted butter, melted

1½ teaspoons vanilla extract

1¼ cups of ¼-inch fresh pineapple pieces

2 cups of ¼-inch banana pieces

Icing

1 medium ripe mango

8 tablespoons (1 stick) unsalted butter, softened

8 ounces cream cheese

1 teaspoon vanilla extract

3 cups confectioners' sugar, sifted

2 tablespoons milk

¼ cup of ¼-inch fresh pineapple pieces

Equipment

Three 9-inch cake pans, buttered and floured

CAKE

Preheat the oven to 350 degrees.

In a large mixing bowl, combine the flour, sugar, salt, baking soda, and cinnamon. Add the eggs and the melted butter, stirring just until combined. Stir in the vanilla, pineapple pieces, and bananas.

Spoon the batter into the three cake pans. Bake until a skewer inserted in the middle comes out clean, about 30 minutes. Cool the cakes in their pans and then unmold them.

ICING

Peel the mango and separate the pulp from the seed. Chop the mango into ¼-inch pieces. Set aside.

Combine the butter, cream cheese, and vanilla. Beat until smooth. Add the confectioners' sugar and mix until combined. Add the milk and mix well.

Place ⅓ of the icing in a mixing bowl and stir in all but ¼ cup of the mango.

Spread half of the mango icing on one of the cakes. Place a second cake on top of the first cake and cover with the rest of the mango icing. Place the third cake on top. Frost the sides and top of the cake with the remaining icing. Place the reserved mango and pineapple pieces on top of the cake.

Refrigerate the cake until you are ready to serve it.

AHEAD-OF-TIME NOTES

The cake layers can be made a day in advance. Store wrapped in plastic wrap at room temperature. The cake can be frosted a day ahead. Refrigerate the finished cake.

GINGER CRÈME "BRÛLÉE"

Traditionally crème brûlées are made with a very thin layer of burnt sugar on top of the custard, hence the name. Here I have substituted a layer of chocolate for the caramel, creating a similar effect.

SERVES 8

1½ cups milk

2¾ cups heavy whipping cream

1 ounce (3-inch piece) fresh ginger, cut into quarters

6 large egg yolks

2 large eggs

¼ cup granulated sugar

Large pinch of salt

2 ounces bittersweet chocolate, finely chopped

Equipment

Eight 4-ounce ramekins

A baking pan large enough to hold all the ramekins

In a medium heavy-bottomed saucepan, scald the milk, cream, and ginger. Remove the pot from the heat, cover it, and let steep for 20 minutes.

In a medium mixing bowl, whisk together the egg yolks, eggs, sugar, and salt.

Remove the cover from the ginger cream. Scald the ginger cream again and slowly whisk it into the egg-sugar mixture. Strain the milk, discarding the ginger. Refrigerate the ginger custard until cold, at least 1 hour.

Preheat the oven to 300 degrees.

Pour the ginger custard into the ramekins. Place the filled ramekins in the large baking pan. Place the baking pan on a rack in the middle of the oven. Carefully fill the baking pan with water so that the water comes halfway up the sides of the ramekins. Cover the pan tightly with aluminum foil. Bake the ginger custards until all but the very centers of the custards are set, about 50 minutes. Refrigerate until firm, about 4 hours.

Melt the chocolate in a double boiler over hot water, making sure that the water does not touch the pan holding the chocolate. Whisk until smooth. With the back of a spoon gently spread a teaspoon of melted chocolate over each ginger custard.

Refrigerate the custards until the chocolate is hard, about 30 minutes.

AHEAD-OF-TIME NOTES

The custard base can be made a couple of days in advance. The ginger crème "brûlées" can be baked a day in advance, but put the chocolate on the day you serve them.

COOKIES AND CANDIES

♦♦♦

Begin the day by dipping a biscotto in your coffee,
nibble on an almond macaroon as an afternoon pick-me-up, and treat
yourself to a white chocolate mint truffle after dinner.
Cookies and candies are the most versatile of all sweets, satisfying
your whim day or night. Serve them as accompaniments to sorbet
or a custard, or offer an assortment and make them dessert by themselves.

WHITE CHOCOLATE RASPBERRY BRITTLE

This artistic garnish can be used on the White Chocolate Mousse with Raspberries (page 59) or on a dessert buffet. Be creative when you swirl the raspberry sauce into the chocolate, making a decorative pattern.

A 10-INCH SQUARE PIECE

8 ounces white chocolate, finely chopped

2 tablespoons Raspberry Purée (page 238), at room temperature

Line a baking tray with parchment paper and set aside.

Melt the chocolate in a double boiler over hot water, making sure that the water does not touch the bottom of the pan holding the chocolate. Whisk until smooth. Using a thin metal spatula, spread the chocolate into a 10-inch square on the baking tray. With a spoon or fork drizzle the raspberry purée over the white chocolate. Swirl the purée into the white chocolate, using the blunt end of a skewer or toothpick.

Let the chocolate brittle set at room temperature for 2 to 3 hours. Peel the parchment paper off the brittle and break the brittle into desired shapes and sizes. The raspberry purée will remain slightly sticky, so handle carefully and do not stack the pieces.

AHEAD-OF-TIME NOTES

This brittle will keep for several days. Store at room temperature.

CARAMEL STRAWBERRIES

These strawberries are a perfect light dessert or, like the candied cranberries, can be used as a garnish on a dessert. Make sure you use strawberries without "white shoulders"—they should be as red and beautiful as possible. If you can, get long-stemmed strawberries, as they are more dramatic and it will be easier to dip them into the caramel.

24 STRAWBERRIES

1 cup granulated sugar
½ cup water
1 tablespoon lemon juice
24 strawberries

In a small heavy-bottomed saucepan, mix together the sugar, water and lemon juice. Cook over medium heat until the sugar dissolves. Increase to high heat and cook the sugar until it is golden amber in color. (Do not stir after you increase the heat.) Remove the caramel from the heat. Holding onto the green top of each strawberry, dip it ¾ of the way into the caramel. Place the coated strawberries on a wire rack. Be careful not to put your fingers into the caramel. (If you drop a strawberry into the caramel take it out with a fork.) Continue dipping the strawberries until all 24 have been coated with the caramel.

Let the caramel harden, about 15 minutes.

Remove the strawberries from the rack by gently pushing them from the stem end until they loosen themselves from the rack.

AHEAD-OF-TIME NOTES

Caramel strawberries are best eaten the day they are made. Store them at room temperature.

REVERSE MOONS

In my first book, Stars Desserts, *Stareos was one of the most popular recipes.*
I've turned Stareos inside out by sandwiching chocolate-flavored mascarpone between vanilla cookies.
I also make them into a crescent moon shape to go side by side with the Stareos.

18 COOKIES

Cookies

¾ *pound (3 sticks) cold unsalted butter*
¾ *cup granulated sugar*
½ *teaspoon vanilla extract*
3 *cups all-purpose flour*

Chocolate Filling

2 *ounces bittersweet chocolate, finely chopped*
1 *cup mascarpone*
1 *tablespoon granulated sugar*
1 *tablespoon cocoa powder*

COOKIES

In the bowl of an electric mixer using the paddle attachment, combine the butter, sugar, and vanilla on low speed for 5 seconds. Add the flour and continue to mix just until the dough comes together, about 5 minutes.

On a lightly floured board roll the dough ¼ inch thick. Cut the dough into crescent moons or any other desired shape. There should be at least 36 cookies. Put the cookies on parchment-paper-lined baking trays and refrigerate for 1 hour.

Preheat the oven to 250 degrees.

Bake the cookies until the centers are firm to the touch, about 1 hour. Let the cookies cool.

CHOCOLATE FILLING

Melt the chocolate in a double boiler over hot water, making sure that the water in the lower part of the double boiler does not touch the bottom of the pan holding the chocolate. Whisk until smooth. Let cool to room temperature.

In a small bowl, combine the sugar, mascarpone, and cocoa powder. Stir in the melted chocolate.

Spread 2 teapoons of the chocolate mascarpone onto 18 of the cookies. Place another cookie on top of the cream. Refrigerate until ready to serve.

AHEAD-OF-TIME NOTES

The cookies and the chocolate mascarpone can each be made a day or two in advance. The sandwiched cookies are best eaten the day they are assembled.

COCONUT HAYSTACKS

These chocolate-covered stacks of coconut look like little piles of hay, hence their name. They are very simple to make. You can substitute milk chocolate for the bittersweet.

12 LARGE OR 24 SMALL HAYSTACKS

2¼ cups flaked sweetened coconut

8 ounces bittersweet chocolate, finely chopped

Preheat the oven to 350 degrees.

Place the coconut in a single layer on a baking tray. Toast until golden brown, about 10 minutes. The edges will toast faster than the middle so stir the coconut every couple of minutes for even coloring.

Melt the chocolate in a double boiler over hot water, making sure that the water does not touch the bottom of the pan holding the chocolate. Remove the chocolate from the heat and whisk until smooth. Stir in the toasted coconut.

Using approximately 1 tablespoon per haystack for large haystacks, form the chocolate and coconut mixture into 1½-inch-tall stacks. Place them on a baking sheet.

Refrigerate until set, about 30 minutes.

AHEAD-OF-TIME NOTES

The coconut haystacks are best eaten the day they are made. Store in the refrigerator.

CHOCOLATE NUT BARK

Chocolate bark can be made with any combination of chocolate and nuts.
I like to make several kinds and put them all together on a platter, contrasting colors, textures,
and tastes. My favorite combinations are white chocolate
and pistachio, bittersweet chocolate and almonds, and milk chocolate and hazelnut.

I POUND OF BARK

1½ cups (6 ounces) whole natural almonds, pistachios, or hazelnuts

8 ounces bittersweet, milk, or white chocolate

Preheat the oven to 350 degrees.

Toast the nuts on a baking tray in the oven. (Toast almonds and hazelnuts for about 15 minutes; pistachios, about 10 minutes. If you are using hazelnuts rub the skins off in a towel after baking.)

Finely chop each type of chocolate separately.

Melt each kind of chocolate separately in a double boiler over hot water, making sure that the water does not touch the bottom of the pan that holds the chocolate. Do not let the chocolate get hot. Remove the chocolate from the heat and whisk until smooth. Cool the chocolate for 5 minutes. Stir one type of nuts into each kind of chocolate you used. Spread the chocolate bark ¼ inch thick onto parchment-lined baking sheets. Let the bark harden, about 6 hours.

Break the chocolate bark up into rough pieces, making them various sizes and shapes.

Refrigerate the chocolate bark.

AHEAD-OF-TIME NOTES

The bark is best eaten the day it is made. Since the chocolate is not tempered it may bloom (get a speckled appearance) the next day. The discoloration will not affect the taste.

MERINGUES

Meringues are fat-free, and that's good, but by themselves they can be somewhat bland.
With a dusting of cocoa powder or instant espresso, they can be brought to life and become one of the few
good-tasting fat-free desserts around!

2 DOZEN 1½-INCH MERINGUES

3 large egg whites
¾ cup granulated sugar
¾ teaspoon cocoa powder

Equipment
A pastry bag fitted with a large tip

Preheat the oven to 225 degrees.

Fill a medium saucepan ¼ full of water. Bring the water to a simmer.

In the bowl of an electric mixer whisk together the egg whites and the sugar. Place the bowl in the saucepan of water and, whisking constantly, heat the egg white mixture until hot. Remove the bowl from the water and put it back on the electric mixer. With the whisk attachment, whip the egg whites on medium high speed until stiff, about 5 minutes.

Place the egg white mixture in a pastry bag fitted with a large pastry tip. (You can use any shape you wish.) Pipe the meringues, 1½ inches wide and 1¾ inches tall, 1 inch apart on parchment-lined baking sheets. Bake until completely dry, 2 hours or more. Cool and dust with the cocoa powder.

AHEAD-OF-TIME NOTES

Meringues will keep a week as long as the weather is not too humid. Store in an airtight container at room temperature.

COFFEE TOFFEE

The addition of coffee to toffee is welcome because it gives the toffee a bitter edge.
Be sure to use a candy thermometer that you can keep in the saucepan during the entire cooking process.

A 9- BY 13-INCH PAN

½ pound (2 sticks) unsalted butter

1 cup granulated sugar

¼ cup plus 2 tablespoons dark brown sugar

¼ cup plus 2 tablespoons water

1 tablespoon molasses

2 teaspoons instant powdered coffee or
  espresso

½ teaspoon ground cinnamon

¼ teaspoon salt

6 ounces bittersweet chocolate, finely chopped

2 ounces white chocolate, finely chopped

Equipment

A 9- by 13-inch pan, buttered

In a medium heavy-bottomed saucepan stir together all of the ingredients except for the bittersweet and white chocolates. Using a candy thermometer, cook the mixture over medium-low heat, stirring frequently, until it reaches 275 degrees. Continue to cook to 315 degrees, stirring constantly.

Quickly remove the saucepan from the heat and whisk until smooth. Pour the mixture into the prepared pan and set aside until hard, about 20 minutes.

Melt the chocolates separately in double boilers over hot water, making sure that the water does not touch the bottom of the pans holding the chocolates. Whisk both chocolates until smooth. Spread the bittersweet chocolate evenly over the toffee. Drizzle the white chocolate over the dark chocolate. Marble the two chocolates together with a toothpick or fork. Let the chocolate harden, about 4 hours.

Cut the toffee into pieces with a sharp knife and remove it from the pan with a narrow metal spatula.

AHEAD-OF-TIME NOTES

This toffee will keep for several days. Store in an airtight container at room temperature.

SUGAR AND SPICE PUMPKIN SEEDS

These are wonderful to snack on while sipping warm apple cider. You can buy hulled pumpkin seeds at health food stores and some grocery stores. If you get the pumpkin seeds out of a pumpkin yourself, make sure you hull and dry them out before using them.

2 1/4 CUPS

6 tablespoons granulated sugar

1 teaspoon ground cinnamon

1/2 teaspoon ground ginger

1 large pinch of grated nutmeg

1 large egg white

2 1/4 cups hulled pumpkin seeds

Preheat the oven to 275 degrees.

In a small bowl, combine the sugar, cinnamon, ginger, and nutmeg. Set aside.

In a separate bowl, whisk the egg white until frothy. Stir in the pumpkin seeds and then the reserved spice mixture. Spread in a single layer on a baking sheet. Bake the seeds for 15 minutes and then stir. Continue to bake the seeds until dry, 10 to 15 more minutes.

AHEAD-OF-TIME NOTES

Sugar and spice pumpkin seeds will last a week. Store at room temperature.

CANDIED CRANBERRY CLUSTERS

These can be enjoyed by themselves or used as a garnish for any fall or winter dessert.

ABOUT 15 CRANBERRY CLUSTERS

½ cup plus 2 tablespoons water

1 cup granulated sugar

1¼ cups cranberries

3 ounces white chocolate, finely chopped

In a small heavy-bottomed saucepan, mix together ½ cup of water and the sugar. Cook over medium heat until the sugar dissolves. Increase to high heat and cook until the sugar is golden amber in color. (Do not stir after you increase the heat.) Remove the caramel from the heat. Carefully stir in the remaining 2 tablespoons of water. Be careful—the caramel is very hot and will sputter as the water is added. Stir the caramel until the bubbles subside. Working quickly, put about 10 cranberries in the caramel. Using 2 forks, coat the cranberries with the caramel. Remove the cranberry cluster (the caramel will make the cranberries stick together), drain off any excess caramel, and put the cluster on a wire rack. Continue with the rest of the cranberries, making one cluster at a time. There should be only a thin layer of caramel coating the cranberries. If the caramel in the pot thickens, making dipping difficult, reheat the caramel for 5 to 10 seconds over medium-low heat.

Let the cranberry clusters set until the caramel hardens, about 15 minutes.

Melt the white chocolate in a double boiler over hot water, making sure that the water does not touch the bottom of the pan holding the chocolate. Whisk the chocolate until smooth. Dip the bottoms of the cranberry clusters into the melted white chocolate. Place on a baking tray and let the white chocolate set.

AHEAD-OF-TIME NOTES

The clusters are best eaten the day they are made. Store at room temperature.

CANDIED CITRUS PEELS

This recipe can be made with orange or lemon peel. I like to make half lemon and half orange so that there are contrasting colors as well as two citrus flavors. It is a very simple recipe, but it does take time, so prepare accordingly.

ABOUT 40 PIECES

1 navel orange

2 lemons

2¼ cups granulated sugar

1½ cups water

1 tablespoon freshly squeezed lemon juice

Cut the orange and lemons in half and juice them. (Save any remaining juice for another use. If you have no immediate need, freeze it.)

Scrape out the fruit membrane of the orange and lemons with a spoon, leaving the shell intact. Cut each half in half. Lay the pieces on a cutting board and slice them lengthwise into ¼-inch pieces.

Fill a medium saucepan with water. Over high heat bring the water to a boil. Add the citrus peels and boil for 5 minutes. Strain the peels and discard the water. Fill the saucepan with fresh water and again bring it to a boil. Add the peels and boil for 5 minutes. Strain. Repeat this process of boiling the citrus peels 2 more times, each time with fresh water. (This removes the bitter flavor from the peels.)

In a clean medium saucepan dissolve 2 cups of the sugar in the 1½ cups water and the lemon juice over medium-low heat. Add the citrus peels and cook until all the peels are translucent, about 1 to 1½ hours.

Strain the citrus peels and place them, so they are not touching, on a wire rack. Let sit overnight to air-dry.

Toss the citrus peels in the remaining ¼ cup sugar, coating them thoroughly.

AHEAD-OF-TIME NOTES

Citrus peels will keep for at least a week. Store in an airtight container at room temperature.

DOUBLE CHOCOLATE BISCOTTI

The biscotti craze is here to stay. Biscotti are almost as popular as chocolate chip cookies.
Biscotti lovers are adamant about what types they prefer and how hard they should be. Chocolate biscotti
are great, but even better when coated in white chocolate.

24 COOKIES

3 large eggs

¾ teaspoon vanilla extract

1⅓ cups all-purpose flour

½ cup cocoa powder

1½ teaspoons baking soda

⅛ teaspoon salt

1 cup granulated sugar

2¼ teaspoons espresso grounds
   or instant espresso

⅔ cup (2 ounces) chocolate chips

1 cup (4 ounces) hazelnuts,
   toasted and skinned

7 ounces white chocolate, finely chopped

Preheat the oven to 325 degrees.

Lightly whisk together the eggs and the vanilla extract. Set aside.

Combine the flour, cocoa powder, baking soda, salt, sugar, espresso grounds, chocolate chips, and hazelnuts in the bowl of an electric mixer. With the paddle attachment, slowly add the egg mixture on low speed. Mix just until the dough comes together. With your hands, scrape any dry ingredients from the bottom of the bowl and mix them into the dough.

On a lightly floured board, roll the dough into 2 logs, each about 12 inches long. Place them on a baking sheet. Bake until the sides are firm and the tops are cracked and no longer wet-looking, about 20 minutes. Cool to room temperature.

Decrease the oven temperature to 300 degrees.

Cut the logs into slices ¾ inch thick. Place them, a cut side up, on a baking sheet. Bake the biscotti until dry and firm, about 25 minutes.

Melt the white chocolate in a double boiler over hot water, making sure that the water does not touch the bottom of the pan holding the chocolate. Whisk until smooth.

Line a baking sheet with parchment paper. Spread some white chocolate on a cut side of each biscotto. Place the biscotti, white chocolate side down, on the baking tray. Let the chocolate harden.

AHEAD-OF-TIME NOTES

Chocolate biscotti will last for about a week. Store in an airtight container at room temperature.

MACADAMIA NUT BISCOTTI

This recipe produces a light delicate biscotto. You can substitute other nuts if you wish.

24 BISCOTTI

1 cup (4 ounces) macadamia nuts

1½ cups all-purpose flour

1½ teaspoons baking powder

¼ teaspoon salt

6 tablespoons (¾ stick) unsalted butter, softened

6 tablespoons granulated sugar

1 large egg

¼ teaspoon vanilla extract

Preheat the oven to 350 degrees.

Toast the macadamia nuts until light brown in color, about 10 minutes. Let cool.

Sift together the flour, baking powder, and salt.

In a food processor, coarsely grind half of the nuts with the flour mixture.

Cream the butter and the sugar until light and fluffy. Add the egg and mix until incorporated. Stir in the vanilla extract and the unground nuts. Add the ground nut mixture.

On a lightly floured board, divide the dough in half. Roll each half into a log 12 inches long. Place the logs on a baking sheet lined with parchment paper. Bake until golden brown in color, about 30 minutes. Let cool.

Decrease the oven temperature to 300 degrees.

Slice the logs at a slight diagonal into ¾ inch slices. Place them cut side up on the baking sheet. Bake until firm, about 15 minutes.

AHEAD-OF-TIME NOTES

These biscotti will last for several days. Store in an airtight container at room temperature.

SPICED ALMONDS

I particularly like these nuts as a garnish to a warm chocolate dessert like the Warm Bittersweet Chocolate Tartlets (page 21), but they are also extraordinary to nibble on by themselves.

4 ¹/₂ CUPS

½ cup firmly packed dark brown sugar

3 tablespoons ground cinnamon

1 large egg white

1 tablespoon vanilla extract

2¾ cups (11 ounces) whole natural almonds

Preheat the oven to 300 degrees.

In a small bowl combine the brown sugar and cinnamon. Set aside.

In a medium-sized bowl, whisk the egg white until frothy. Stir in the vanilla extract, almonds, and the reserved brown sugar mixture.

Spread the almonds in a single layer on a baking sheet and bake them, stirring every 10 minutes, until they are dry, about 30 minutes.

AHEAD-OF-TIME NOTES

Spiced almonds will last at least a week if stored in an airtight container at room temperature.

HAZELNUT CHOCOLATE FUDGE

This is one of the easiest candy recipes around.

1 cup sweetened condensed milk

1 pound bittersweet chocolate, coarsely chopped

1 tablespoon vanilla extract

2 cups (8 ounces) hazelnuts, toasted and skinned

Equipment

A 9- by 9-inch pan, buttered

Combine the condensed milk, chocolate, and vanilla extract in the top of a double boiler. Melt the mixture, making sure that the water does not touch the bottom of the pan holding the chocolate. (Do not let the mixture get hot or the fudge will be grainy.) Stir the chocolate mixture until smooth. Stir in the hazelnuts. Spread the fudge in the prepared pan. Let it harden about 2 hours and then cut into 1-inch pieces.

AHEAD-OF-TIME NOTES

The fudge will keep for several days. Store in an airtight container at room temperature.

COCONUT SESAME COOKIES

This recipe comes from Joyce Orenstein, the mother of my friend (and fellow pastry chef) Julia Orenstein.
These cookies are incredible with a tropical fruit compote of pineapples, papaya, mangoes, and bananas.

36 COOKIES

14 tablespoons (1¼ sticks) unsalted butter,
   softened

⅔ cup granulated sugar

1¼ cups all-purpose flour

⅓ cup plus 1 tablespoon sesame seeds

¾ cup shredded sweetened coconut

¼ cup (1 ounce) sliced almonds, toasted

Preheat the oven to 350 degrees.

In the bowl of an electric mixer using the paddle attachment, cream the butter and sugar. Add the flour, ⅓ cup sesame seeds, coconut, and almonds. Mix just until incorporated.

On a lightly floured board, roll the dough in a log about 18 inches long. Refrigerate the dough until firm. Slice the log ⅜ inch thick.

Place the cookies 2½ inches apart on a parchment-paper-lined baking sheet. Sprinkle the remaining tablespoon of sesame seeds on top of the cookies. Bake until golden brown around the edges, about 20 minutes.

AHEAD-OF-TIME NOTES

The cookies will keep for several days. Store in an airtight container at room temperature.

ALMOND MACAROONS

*Traditionally, almond macaroons are made with ground almonds or almond paste.
I like to use sliced almonds instead, which gives the cookies additional texture and crunch.*

ABOUT 20 COOKIES

3 cups (12 ounces) sliced almonds, toasted
1¼ cups granulated sugar
½ cup (about 4) egg whites
1 tablespoon honey
¾ teaspoon vanilla extract
¼ teaspoon almond extract
½ cup all-purpose flour
Pinch of salt

In a food processor, finely grind ⅓ cup of the sliced almonds with the sugar. Set aside.

Lightly beat the egg whites until frothy, and then stir in the ground almond-sugar mixture, honey, vanilla extract, and almond extract.

Heat the egg white mixture in a double boiler over simmering water, stirring frequently, until hot. Remove the mixture from the stove and stir in the flour, salt and the remaining 2⅔ cups sliced almonds. Refrigerate the almond mixture for 2 hours until cold.

Preheat the oven to 325 degrees.

Using 1½ tablespoons of batter for each macaroon, place them 2 inches apart on parchment-lined baking trays.

Bake until golden brown, 10 to 15 minutes. Cool the macaroons and then remove them from the baking trays.

AHEAD-OF-TIME NOTES

Almond macaroons will keep for several days. Store in an airtight container at room temperature.

MACADAMIA NUT BRITTLE

Made like traditional peanut brittle, this macadamia nut brittle is a new twist on an old theme.
If you cannot find unsalted macadamia nuts, use salted and omit the salt in the recipe.

ABOUT 1 POUND

¾ teaspoon baking soda

⅛ teaspoon salt

½ cup light corn syrup

1 cup granulated sugar

1 cup (4 ounces) macadamia nuts,
    coarsely chopped

½ teaspoon vanilla extract

4 tablespoons (½ stick) unsalted butter,
    softened

Equipment

Candy thermometer

An 11- by 17-inch baking tray, buttered

In a small bowl, mix together the baking soda and salt. Set aside.

In a 2½-quart heavy-bottomed saucepan, combine the corn syrup and the sugar. Bring the mixture to a boil over medium-high heat and cook to 255 degrees on the candy thermometer. Carefully stir in the macadamia nuts and continue to cook the mixture, stirring constantly, to 300 degrees on the candy thermometer.

Remove the saucepan from the heat and stir in the reserved baking soda and salt.

Stir in the vanilla extract and the butter, mixing until the butter is completely incorporated. Pour the brittle across the buttered baking tray. Tilt and rotate the pan, letting the brittle spread as thinly as possible over the baking tray.

(To clean the saucepan and thermometer: Fill the saucepan with water, insert the thermometer, and bring it to a boil. This will loosen any hard pieces sticking to the saucepan and thermometer.)

Let the brittle cool to room temperature and then crack it into small pieces.

AHEAD-OF-TIME NOTES

This brittle will keep for at least a week. Store in an airtight container at room temperature.

PISTACHIO TUILES

You can use any kind of nuts in this recipe. I like to use pistachios and serve them
with the Tangerine Ice (page 159). Tuiles are very fragile, so I've allowed extra batter in case some break.

ABOUT 2 DOZEN COOKIES

¾ cup (3 ounces) pistachios, toasted

¾ cup plus 1 tablespoon granulated sugar

3 large egg whites

9 tablespoons (1 stick plus 1 tablespoon)
  unsalted butter, melted and cooled
  to room temperature

½ teaspoon vanilla extract

¾ cup plus 1½ tablespoons all-purpose flour

1½ teaspoons finely chopped lemon zest

Preheat the oven to 350 degrees.

In a food processor, finely grind the pistachios with the sugar. Set aside.

In a medium bowl, whisk the egg whites just until frothy. Stir in the pistachio mixture and then the melted butter and vanilla extract. Stir in the flour and the lemon zest.

Using 2 teaspoons of the batter for each tuile, spread the batter into 3-inch circles on parchment-lined baking sheets, leaving 1 inch between the tuiles. Bake for about 10 minutes until lightly golden. Using a thin metal spatula, quickly take one of the tuiles off the baking sheet. Place the tuile upside down on the work surface and roll it into a wide cylinder. Continue with the other tuiles in the same manner. The tuiles must be rolled while they are hot or they will crack and break. If the tuiles cool and get crisp before you have a chance to roll them, put them back in the oven for 15 to 30 seconds to soften. (The cookies can also be served in unrolled flat circles.)

AHEAD-OF-TIME NOTES

The tuiles will keep for a couple of days. Store in an airtight container at room temperature. (If they get soggy on the second day put them in a preheated 350-degree oven for a couple of minutes to recrisp them.)

SNAPPY GINGERSNAPS

These gingersnaps are crisp, full of spicy ginger flavor, and should be dipped in a glass of milk!

APPROXIMATELY 3¹/₂ DOZEN

½ pound (2 sticks) unsalted butter, softened

1½ cups granulated sugar

1 large egg

¼ cup molasses

4 teaspoons ground ginger

1½ tablespoons grated fresh ginger

2 teaspoons baking soda

¼ teaspoon salt

2¼ cups all-purpose flour

Preheat the oven to 350 degrees.

In the bowl of an electric mixer using the paddle attachment, beat the butter and sugar on medium speed until light and creamy. Add the egg and then the molasses. Mix until combined. Decrease to low speed and mix in the ground ginger, grated ginger, baking soda, salt, and flour. Do not overmix.

Using about 1 tablespoon of dough for each cookie, roll into 1 inch balls, placing them 2 inches apart on parchment-lined baking sheets. Bake until flat and evenly brown, about 13 minutes. Cool and then remove the cookies from the baking trays.

AHEAD-OF-TIME NOTES

These gingersnaps will keep for several days, though they are best eaten the day they are baked. Store in an airtight container at room temperature.

MARMALADE WINDOW COOKIES

*The addition of lemon zest and orange marmalade to this simple butter cookie creates
something quite sophisticated.*

ABOUT 24 COOKIES

½ pound (2 sticks) unsalted butter, softened

1 cup granulated sugar

1 teaspoon finely chopped lemon zest

2 large eggs

½ teaspoon vanilla extract

4 cups all-purpose flour

½ cup good-quality orange marmalade
   (preferably nonchunky)

In the bowl of an electric mixer combine the butter, sugar, and lemon zest. With the paddle attachment, beat the mixture on medium speed until smooth and creamy. Add the eggs and vanilla extract and mix well. Decrease to low speed and add the flour, mixing until combined. Form the dough into a ball and refrigerate for at least an hour until firm, but not so hard that it cannot be rolled.

Preheat the oven to 350 degrees.

On a lightly floured board, roll the dough ⅛ inch thick. Using a fluted pastry wheel, cut the dough into 2-inch squares. Reroll the dough scraps and continue cutting out 2 inch squares until you have 48 pieces.

With a small decorative cutter, cut out the centers of 24 of the cookies.

Place the cookie squares ¼ inch apart on parchment-paper-lined baking sheets. Bake the cookies until golden brown around the edges, about 15 minutes. (If you like, bake the decorative cutouts along with the cookie squares. Enjoy them as mini cookies to nibble on.) Let the cookies cool.

Place 1 teaspoon of marmalade in the center of each of the solid cookie squares. Gently press the cutout cookies on top of the marmalade-spread cookies.

AHEAD-OF-TIME NOTES

These cookies are best eaten the day they are assembled. The cookies can be baked a day before you assemble them. Store in an airtight container at room temperature.

SUGARED PEANUTS

These peanuts are a nice garnish for the Chocolate Peanut Butter Terrine (page 40), or on their own on a dessert buffet. Be careful—they are very addicting!

2 CUPS

2 large egg whites
¾ cup granulated sugar
2 cups shelled unsalted peanuts

Preheat the oven to 350 degrees.

In a medium bowl whisk the egg whites until frothy. Stir in the sugar. Add the peanuts and mix until well combined.

Spread the peanuts in a single layer on a baking sheet. Roast the peanuts, stirring them every 5 minutes, until they are dry and golden brown, 15 to 20 minutes.

AHEAD-OF-TIME NOTES

Sugared peanuts will keep for several days. Store in an airtight container at room temperature.

ALMOND PRALINE

Almond praline can be enjoyed many ways: by itself in 1-inch pieces; chopped and served with Baked Apricots (page 90), or as a garnish with your favorite chocolate cake.

ABOUT I POUND

½ cup water

1½ cups granulated sugar

1 cup (4 ounces) whole natural almonds, toasted

Equipment

A 17- by 11-inch baking sheet

Butter the bottom of the baking sheet. Set aside.

In a medium heavy-bottomed saucepan, mix together the water and sugar. Cook over medium heat until the sugar dissolves. Increase to high heat and cook the sugar until it is golden amber in color. (Do not stir after you increase the heat.) Remove the saucepan from the heat, let the bubbles subside, and carefully stir in the almonds. Pour the mixture into the buttered pan. Let the mixture harden, about one hour.

Gently tap the almond praline against the counter to loosen it from the pan. Break it into pieces with your hands. If you are using the almond praline as a garnish, coarsely grind it in a food processor using quick on-off turns.

AHEAD-OF-TIME NOTES

The praline will keep for a week, depending upon the humidity. Store in an airtight container at room temperature.

WHITE CHOCOLATE MINT TRUFFLES

White chocolate is the best type of chocolate to combine with mint. Its flavor is softer than that of dark chocolate, and therefore the flavor pairs more evenly with mint.

ABOUT 35 TRUFFLES, 1 INCH EACH

1 pound 10 ounces white chocolate
½ cup heavy whipping cream
¼ cup loosely packed mint leaves
1½ ounces bittersweet chocolate

Finely chop 1 pound of the white chocolate and place it in a medium bowl. Set aside.

In a small heavy-bottomed saucepan, scald the cream over medium-high heat. Remove the cream from the heat and add the mint leaves. Set aside for 15 minutes to steep. Strain the cream and discard the mint. Return the mint-flavored cream to the saucepan. Scald the cream again and pour it over the chopped white chocolate. Whisk until smooth. Refrigerate until firm, 2 to 3 hours.

For each truffle, scoop about 1 teaspoon of the white chocolate mixture and, with your hands, roll it into a ball. Scoop and roll all of the white chocolate mixture. Refrigerate until firm, 1 to 2 hours.

Melt the remaining 10 ounces of white chocolate in a double boiler over hot water, making sure that the water does not touch the bottom of the pan that holds the chocolate. Whisk until smooth. Dip each of the balls in the white chocolate. Remove them with a fork, allowing any excess chocolate to drop off. Refrigerate until firm, about 30 minutes.

Melt the bittersweet chocolate in a double boiler over hot water, making sure that the water does not touch the bottom of the pan holding the chocolate. Whisk until smooth. With the tines of a fork, drizzle the bittersweet chocolate over the white chocolate truffles.

AHEAD-OF-TIME NOTES

The truffles will keep for several days. Store in the refrigerator.

CHOCOLATE-DIPPED PEANUT BUTTER COOKIES

There are already numerous recipes for peanut butter cookies, and yet I could not resist adding just one more. This recipe will make you forsake all others, especially once you taste them dipped in chocolate. The only peanut butter cookie better than this one is a Girl Scout peanut butter patty!

3 DOZEN COOKIES

2 cups all-purpose flour

½ teaspoon baking soda

¼ teaspoon salt

10 tablespoons (1¼ sticks) unsalted butter, softened

1 cup creamy peanut butter

⅔ cup granulated sugar

1 cup dark firmly packed brown sugar

2 large eggs

½ teaspoon vanilla extract

8 ounces bittersweet chocolate, finely chopped

Preheat the oven to 350 degrees.

Sift together the flour, baking soda, and salt. Set aside.

Cream the butter, peanut butter, granulated sugar, and brown sugar. Add the eggs and vanilla extract.

Stir in the dry ingredients. Mix just until the flour is incorporated. Do not overmix.

Roll the dough into 1½-inch balls and place them 2 inches apart on parchment-lined baking sheets. Press with a fork to flatten them slightly and to make a crosshatch pattern.

Bake the cookies until firm around the edges but still soft in the center, about 15 minutes.

Melt the chocolate in a double boiler over hot water, making sure that the water does not touch the bottom of the pan holding the chocolate. Whisk until smooth. Dip each cookie halfway into the chocolate. Place on a wire rack and refrigerate the cookies until set.

AHEAD-OF-TIME NOTES

These cookies, like all cookies, are best the first day. Store in the refrigerator.

ORANGE PECAN FLORENTINES

I prefer pecans in florentines because they have a much stronger, richer flavor than florentines made in the traditional manner with almonds.

24 COOKIES

¾ cup granulated sugar

¾ cup (3 ounces) pecan pieces, toasted

4 tablespoons (½ stick) unsalted butter

2 tablespoons honey

2½ tablespoons light corn syrup

3½ tablespoons heavy whipping cream

1 tablespoon finely chopped orange zest

3 ounces bittersweet chocolate, finely chopped

Preheat the oven to 350 degrees.

In a food processor, finely grind the sugar and the pecans.

In a medium heavy-bottomed saucepan, combine the pecan mixture with the butter, honey, light corn syrup, cream, and orange zest. Cook over medium heat until the sugar is dissolved and the ingredients are well blended, 2 to 3 minutes. The batter will be thin.

While the mixture is still hot, using 1 teaspoon of batter for each, place the florentines 3 inches apart on parchment-lined baking sheets. There should be 48 cookies. Bake the florentines for 3 to 5 minutes until golden brown. Let them cool to room temperature.

Melt the chocolate in a double boiler over hot water, making sure that the water does not touch the bottom of the pan holding the chocolate. Whisk until smooth. Spread the chocolate on 24 of the florentines. Place a second florentine over each of those spread with chocolate to make sandwiches. Let the chocolate set.

AHEAD-OF-TIME NOTES

The florentines are best eaten the day they are made. Store them in an airtight container at room temperature.

KEY RECIPES,
CREAMS, AND SAUCES

♦♦♦

The doughs, creams, and sauces in this chapter are fundamental
recipes necessary to many of the desserts. I am compiling them in their own
chapter for handy reference. The puff pastry, the pie and
tart doughs, and the trifle cakes should be a part of your basic baking
repertoire. Use your imagination when deciding which sauces
or creams to use with a particular dessert — the possibilities are limitless.

WHIPPED CREAM

Some purists believe that cream should only be whipped by hand, as the texture and therefore the experience is much better. I wouldn't necessarily go that far, but it is crucial that the cream not be over-whipped, even just a little bit. Overwhipped cream, even when just served on the side, can ruin a dessert. If you overwhip the cream, fold in a few tablespoons of unwhipped cream. Do not use ultrapasteurized cream unless there is no alternative. It does not hold a whip well, and produces a much thinner whipped cream. Whenever I have to use ultrapasteurized cream I add a little sour cream before whipping, making it thicker.

ABOUT 3 CUPS

1½ cups heavy whipping cream

1 teaspoon vanilla extract

1 tablespoon granulated sugar

In a bowl combine the cream, vanilla extract, and sugar. Whip until soft peaks form. The cream should have a satiny appearance. It should not be grainy.

HALF-WHIPPED CREAM

I enjoy the taste and feel (in my mouth) of half-whipped cream. Whip just enough to hold its shape.

2½ CUPS

1½ cups heavy whipping cream

1 teaspoon vanilla extract

1 tablespoon granulated sugar

In a bowl combine the cream, vanilla extract, and sugar. Whip cream just enough to hold its shape.

AHEAD-OF-TIME NOTES

Whipped cream and half-whipped cream should be prepared within an hour of serving. Store in the rerigerator. When whipped cream sits, the water separates from the rest of the cream in the bottom of the bowl. If this happens, whisk until smooth.

TART AND PIE DOUGHS

Here are two all-purpose tart and pie doughs. As with all doughs, be careful not to overmix them. Rolling out dough should be easy. If it is a hot day, make sure that the dough is well chilled so that it won't stick to the rolling pin or the work surface. If the dough is too hard, let it soften at room temperature for a few minutes before you try to roll it or it will crack. Don't fight with the dough; it will always win.

ONE 9½-INCH TART OR SIX 4-INCH WIDE BY 1-INCH HIGH TARTLETS
ONE 9-INCH SINGLE-CRUST PIE

Tart Dough

1 large egg

1½ tablespoons heavy whipping cream

2 cups all-purpose flour

1½ tablespoons granulated sugar

Pinch of salt

12 tablespoons (1½ sticks) cold unsalted
    butter

TART DOUGH

In a small bowl, mix together the egg and cream. Set aside.

In the bowl of an electric mixer, combine the flour, sugar, salt, and butter. Using the paddle attachment on low speed, mix in the butter until it is the size of small peas. With the mixer on low speed, add the egg mixture. Mix the dough just until it is no longer dry-looking. It will still be loose and crumbly at this point.

Place the dough on the work surface. With your hands, combine and form the dough into a single ball. Wrap the dough in plastic wrap and refrigerate until firm but still malleable.

Pie Dough

1⅔ cups all-purpose flour

Pinch of salt

1 tablespoon granulated sugar

14 tablespoons (1¾ sticks) cold
    unsalted butter

2 tablespoons cold water

PIE DOUGH

In the bowl of an electric mixer, combine the flour, salt, sugar, and butter. Using the paddle attachment on low speed, mix in the butter until it is the size of small peas. With the mixer on low speed, add the water, mixing just until the dough is no longer dry looking. (The amount of water given here is approximate. You may need a little more. Add the amount listed and if the dough is still dry, add a teaspoon or two more. Be careful not to add too much or the dough will be tough.)

With your hands, combine the dough and form it into a single ball. Wrap the dough in plastic wrap and refrigerate for 30 minutes.

ROLLING AND FORMING THE SHELLS

On a lightly floured work surface roll the dough out to the specified thickness. For tart shells: $\frac{3}{16}$ inch thick; for tartlet shells: $\frac{1}{8}$ inch thick; for pie shells: $\frac{1}{4}$ inch thick; for lattice: $\frac{3}{16}$-inch thick and cut into $\frac{1}{2}$-inch strips.

When lining tart and pie pans, be sure to press the dough carefully around the bottom edges of the pans. For prebaked pie shells and pies using lattice, make a decorative edge on the pie shell. If making a 2-crust pie, leave the edge flat.

PREBAKING SHELLS

To prebake a frozen or chilled shell line it with parchment paper. Fill the shell with uncooked rice, beans, or pie weights. (This helps the shell retain its shape.) Bake the shell in a preheated 350-degree oven until the edges are golden brown, about 20 minutes. Remove the parchment paper and the rice, beans, or weights and continue to bake the shell until it is golden brown all over, about 10 minutes more.

GENERAL INFORMATION

1. To make a 2-crust pie, double the pie dough recipe.

2. To make enough lattice for 1 tart or pie, prepare $\frac{1}{2}$ of either recipe.

AHEAD-OF-TIME NOTES

Unbaked shells can be stored for a day in the refrigerator or for several weeks in the freezer. Once a shell is baked, it should be eaten that day for maximum freshness and flakiness of the crust.

PLUM CARAMEL SAUCE

Feel free to substitute peach, rhubarb, or apricot purée for the plums. Serve with the Hazelnut Shortcake (page 99) or the Plum Vanilla Bombe (page 104).

ABOUT 3 CUPS

1½ pounds plums
1 cup granulated sugar
½ cup water

Halve and pit the plums. In a food processor, purée them. Strain the purée to eliminate any skin. Set aside.

In a medium saucepan, stir together the sugar and the water. Cook over medium heat until the sugar dissolves. Increase to high heat and cook the mixture until it is golden amber in color. (Do not stir after you increase the heat.) Remove the saucepan from the heat and stir a few tablespoons of the plum purée into the caramel. (Be careful—the caramel will sputter as the plum purée is added.) Let the caramel bubble and subside and then add a few more tablespoons of plum purée. Slowly add the rest of the plum purée.

Refrigerate until ready to serve.

AHEAD-OF-TIME NOTES

The sauce can be made a day or two in advance.

CARAMEL RUM RAISIN SAUCE

You can vary the dried fruit and serve this sauce with everything from almond cake to ice cream or baked apples.

ABOUT 3 CUPS

3 cups granulated sugar
1 cup water
¾ cup heavy whipping cream
½ cup dark rum
1 cup raisins

In a medium saucepan, stir together the sugar and water. Cook over medium heat until the sugar dissolves. Increase to high heat and cook the mixture until it is golden amber in color. (Do not stir after you increase the heat.) Remove the saucepan from the heat and stir in a few tablespoons of the cream. Let the caramel bubble and subside and then add a few more tablespoons of cream. Be careful—the caramel will sputter as the cream is added. Slowly add the rest of the cream. Stir in the rum. Mix until well combined and stir in the raisins.

Serve the sauce warm. It can be reheated in a double boiler.

AHEAD-OF-TIME NOTES

The sauce can be made a day or two in advance. Store in the refrigerator.

APPLE CARAMEL SAUCE

This sauce was created for the Pumpkin Soufflé (page 132) but can be enjoyed with any fall dessert.

2 CUPS

1½ cups granulated sugar

¾ cup water

1 cup apple juice

In a medium saucepan, stir together the sugar and water. Cook over medium heat until the sugar dissolves. Increase to high heat and cook the mixture until it is golden amber in color. (Do not stir after you increase the heat.) Remove the saucepan from the heat and stir in a few tablespoons of the apple juice. Let the caramel bubble and subside and then add a few more tablespoons of apple juice. Be careful—the caramel will sputter as the apple juice is added. Slowly add the rest of the apple juice.

Let the sauce cool to room temperature and then serve.

AHEAD-OF-TIME NOTES

The sauce can be made a day or two in advance. Store in the refrigerator.

ESPRESSO CARAMEL SAUCE

Serve this with the Bittersweet Chocolate Soufflé (page 47) or any chocolate cake.

2 ½ CUPS

2¼ cups granulated sugar

¾ cup water

½ cup liquid espresso, at room temperature

1 cup heavy whipping cream

In a medium saucepan, stir together the sugar and water. Cook over medium heat until the sugar dissolves. Increase to high heat and cook the mixture until it is golden amber in color. (Do not stir after you increase the heat.) Remove the saucepan from the heat and add a few tablespoons of espresso. Let the caramel bubble and subside and then add a few more tablespoons of espresso. Be careful—the caramel will sputter as the espresso is added. Slowly add the rest of the espresso. Stir in the cream.

Serve the sauce warm. It can be reheated in a double boiler.

AHEAD-OF-TIME NOTES

The sauce can be made a day or two in advance. Store in the refrigerator.

CARAMEL SAUCE

This caramel sauce can be served as is or used as a flavoring in many sauces.

ABOUT 1½ CUPS

1½ cups granulated sugar
½ cup water
1 cup heavy whipping cream

In a medium saucepan, stir together the sugar and the water. Cook over medium heat until the sugar dissolves. Increase to high heat and cook the mixture until it is golden amber in color. (Do not stir after you increase the heat.) Remove the saucepan from the heat and carefully stir in a few tablespoons of cream. Let the caramel bubble and subside and then add a few more tablespoons of cream. Slowly add the rest of the cream. Stir until smooth.

Serve the sauce warm or cold. It can be reheated in a double boiler.

AHEAD-OF-TIME NOTES

The sauce can be made several days in advance. Store in the refrigerator.

CHOCOLATE CARAMEL SAUCE

Here two very popular flavors are combined into one incredible sauce.

2 CUPS

3 ounces bittersweet chocolate
1½ cups warm Caramel Sauce (above)

Finely chop the chocolate. Melt the chocolate in a double boiler over hot water, making sure that the water does not touch the pan holding the chocolate. Whisk until smooth.

Whisk the chocolate into the caramel sauce.

Serve the sauce warm or cold. It can be reheated in a double boiler.

AHEAD-OF-TIME NOTES

The sauce can be made a day or two in advance. Store in the refrigerator.

HOT FUDGE RUM SAUCE

This is a variation of a sauce my grandmother made for my brothers and sister and me.
Hers did not have any rum in it—but I was only about six years old!

ABOUT 3 CUPS

4 ounces unsweetened chocolate

2 tablespoons unsalted butter

¾ cup granulated sugar

1 cup heavy whipping cream

¼ cup dark rum

Melt the chocolate and butter in a double boiler over hot water, making sure that the water does not touch the pan holding the chocolate. Whisk until smooth. Stir in the cream and then the sugar. Cook, stirring frequently, until the sauce slightly thickens and heavily coats the back of a spoon, about 10 to 15 minutes. Stir in the rum.

Serve the sauce warm. It can be reheated in a double boiler.

AHEAD-OF-TIME NOTES

The sauce can be made a day or two in advance. Store in the refrigerator.

BUTTERSCOTCH SAUCE

My mother is a real butterscotch fan. She once told me that I had to include a butterscotch sauce recipe in my book or she wouldn't buy it! This sauce is good on anything.

ABOUT 2 CUPS

8 tablespoons (1 stick) unsalted butter

⅔ cup firmly packed dark brown sugar

⅔ cup granulated sugar

2 tablespoons water

¾ cup light corn syrup

5 tablespoons heavy whipping cream

In a small heavy-bottomed saucepan melt the butter. Stir in the brown and granulated sugars, water, and corn syrup. Bring to a boil over medium heat. Boil for 2 minutes. Cool for 15 minutes and then whisk in the cream.

Serve the sauce warm or cold. It can be reheated in a double boiler.

AHEAD-OF-TIME NOTES

The butterscotch sauce can be made a day or two in advance. Store in the refrigerator.

VANILLA CRÈME ANGLAISE

*The flavor possibilities of crème anglaise are endless. Nuts, citrus peel,
or espresso can be infused in the milk. Liqueurs, chocolate, or berry purées can be stirred in after cooking.
This recipe is a good base for almost any flavor you create.*

ABOUT 2 CUPS

8 large egg yolks
5 tablespoons granulated sugar
Pinch of salt
2½ cups milk
½ vanilla bean

Fill a medium bowl ⅓ full of ice water. Set aside.

In a medium mixing bowl whisk together the egg yolks, sugar, and salt.

Put the milk in a medium heavy-bottomed saucepan. Cut the vanilla bean in half lengthwise, scrape out the insides of the bean and add the entire bean to the milk. Scald the milk over medium-high heat. Slowly whisk it into the reserved egg mixture. Return the milk mixture to the pot and cook the mixture over medium heat, stirring constantly until it coats the back of a spoon, about 5 minutes.

Pour the custard sauce back into the mixing bowl. Place the bowl in the bowl of ice water. Stir occasionally until cold, and then strain.

Refrigerate until ready to serve.

AHEAD-OF-TIME NOTES

Crème anglaise can be made a day or two in advance. Store in the refrigerator.

PUMPKIN PURÉE

Pumpkin purée has a much fresher flavor than canned pumpkin. Use small sugar pumpkins, not the large jack-o'-lantern variety.

ABOUT I CUP

1¼ pounds sugar pumpkin

3 tablespoons water

Preheat the oven to 350 degrees.

Cut the pumpkin into sixths. Scrape out the seeds, saving them for the Sugar and Spice Pumpkin Seeds (page 199).

Put the pumpkin pieces and the water in a baking pan. Cover the pan with aluminum foil and bake until soft, about 1 hour and 15 minutes.

Scoop the flesh from the pumpkin. In a food processor purée the flesh until smooth. Refrigerate until ready to use.

AHEAD-OF-TIME NOTES

Pumpkin purée can be made several days in advance. Store in the refrigerator. It also freezes well.

SWEET POTATO PURÉE

Sweet potatoes shouldn't be limited to side dishes. Use this purée in the Sweet Potato Pumpkin Tart (page 144) or even folded with egg whites and made into a soufflé.

ABOUT I ½ CUPS

2 sweet potatoes

3 tablespoons water

Preheat the oven to 350 degrees.

Prick the sweet potatoes with a fork. Place on a roasting pan and bake the sweet potatoes until soft, about 1 hour.

Scoop the sweet potato pulp from the skins. Mix until smooth.

Refrigerate until ready to use.

AHEAD-OF-TIME NOTES

Sweet potato purée can be made several days in advance. Store in the refrigerator. It also freezes well.

PUFF PASTRY

In most recipes you only need about 1 pound of puff pastry. This is for a larger quantity,
so you will have some ready any time you may want it.
Serve baked puff pastry with fresh fruit and a sauce and you have a superb last-minute dessert.

3 POUNDS OF PUFF PASTRY

2¾ cups all-purpose flour

1 cup cake flour

1¼ teaspoons salt

1 pound plus 8 tablespoons (5 sticks)
  unsalted butter, at room temperature

2 tablespoons freshly squeezed lemon juice

¾ cup plus 2 tablespoons ice water

In a medium mixing bowl, stir together the all-purpose and cake flours and salt. Remove ½ cup and set aside.

In the bowl of an electric mixer using the paddle attachment on low speed, combine 12 tablespoons (1½ sticks) butter with the remaining flour. Combine just until the mixture has the texture of coarse meal.

Combine the lemon juice and water and add to the flour and butter mixture. Mix until the dough comes together and is slightly sticky.

With your hands, shape the dough into a 4-inch square. Wrap the dough in plastic wrap and refrigerate for 45 minutes.

In the bowl of an electric mixer using the paddle attachment on medium-low speed, beat the remaining (3½ sticks) butter until soft and smooth. Add the reserved ½ cup flour and beat until incorporated. Wrap the butter in plastic wrap. With your hands, shape the butter into a 6-inch square. Refrigerate until cold but still pliable, about 45 minutes.

Remove the 4-inch square of dough from the refrigerator. Place it on a lightly floured board and roll it into a 13-inch square. Put the 6-inch square of butter in the middle of the dough. Turn the edges of the dough over the butter, completely covering the butter block.

Roll the dough into a 19- by 6½-inch rectangle. Fold the dough toward the center in thirds as you would a business letter. Turn the dough so that the seam is on the left and the "open" end is on the right. Roll and fold the dough one more time in the same manner. The dough has now been given 2 turns. Refrigerate the dough for 1 hour.

Remove the dough from the refrigerator. Roll and fold the dough 2 times as before. Refrigerate the dough for 1 hour.

Once again, remove the dough from the refrigerator. Roll and fold the dough 2 more times. Refrigerate the dough for 1 hour.

The puff pastry is now ready to be rolled as required in each recipe. See individual recipes for instructions, noting the weight specified and cutting off (and weighing on a kitchen scale) the correct amount.

AHEAD-OF-TIME NOTES

Puff pastry can be made several days in advance, and can be frozen for several weeks. Store well wrapped in plastic wrap. Defrost overnight in the refrigerator before rolling. If possible, roll out the pastry on a lightly floured work surface in desired shapes before freezing. In this instance, place the pastry pieces in the oven directly from the freezer.

Puff pastry should be eaten the same day it is baked.

CARAMEL CRÈME FRAÎCHE

This is one of my favorite sauces. The tang of the crème fraîche pairs very well with the sweetness of the caramel. Crème fraîche is now available in many grocery stores.

ABOUT 2 CUPS

1 cup crème fraîche
¼ cup cold Caramel Sauce (page 230)

In the bowl of an electric mixer combine the crème fraîche and the caramel sauce. Using the whisk attachment, whip the mixture on high speed until thick.

Refrigerate until ready to serve.

AHEAD-OF-TIME NOTES

This is best made and served on the same day. If it is made more than 6 hours in advance, it may need to be rewhipped.

BROWN SUGAR CRÈME FRAÎCHE

Crème fraîche becomes very thin when you add ingredients to it. Therefore, I find it much easier to whip it in a machine rather than by hand.

ABOUT 1 ½ CUPS

1½ cups crème fraîche
¼ cup firmly packed dark brown sugar

In the bowl of an electric mixer combine the crème fraîche and brown sugar. Using the whisk attachment, whip the mixture on high speed until thick.

Refrigerate until ready to serve.

AHEAD-OF-TIME NOTES

This is best made and served on the same day. If it is made more than 6 hours in advance, it may need to be rewhipped.

VANILLA GENOISE

Feel free to add spices or citrus zest to this cake recipe. It's great for trifles and any recipe where the cake needs to be soaked. It is easier to cut this cake for trifles and for the Raspberry Champagne Cream Cake (page 73) if it is a day old.

AN 11- BY 17- BY 1-INCH CAKE

6 large eggs, separated

1½ cups granulated sugar

½ teaspoon salt

1 teaspoon vanilla extract

¼ cup hot water

4 tablespoons (½ stick) unsalted butter, melted

1 cup all-purpose flour

Equipment

An 11- by 17- by 1-inch baking tray, the bottom lined with parchment paper

Preheat the oven to 350 degrees.

In the bowl of an electric mixer, combine the egg yolks, 1 cup of the sugar, the salt, and vanilla. Using the whisk attachment on high speed whip until thick, 3 to 5 minutes. Reduce to medium speed and slowly add the hot water. Scrape down the sides of the bowl. Increase to high speed and again whip until thick. Fold in the flour and then the melted butter. Set aside.

In a clean bowl of an electric mixer using the whisk attachment, whip the egg whites on medium speed until frothy. Increase to high speed and slowly add the remaining ½ cup sugar. Whip the egg whites until stiff and then fold them into the reserved batter. Gently spread the batter in the prepared baking tray. Bake until the cake is golden brown and springs back lightly when touched, about 20 to 25 minutes.

Cool the cake in the pan. Remove the cake from the pan by running a knife along the inside edge of the pan and inverting it onto a work surface. Carefully peel off the parchment paper.

AHEAD-OF-TIME NOTES

The genoise can be made a day or two in advance. Store wrapped in plastic wrap at room temperature. It also freezes well.

BERRY PURÉE

Some recipes call for sweetened berry purée and some for unsweetened. Use this recipe
as your base and add sugar as required. Any berries can be substituted. Taste the purée before adding sugar,
as the sweetness of the fruit varies. The yield may vary as berries have different juice contents.

4 cups raspberries, strawberries or blackberries
Pinch of salt
(6 tablespoons granulated sugar)

In a food processor, purée the berries. Strain the purée through a strainer to eliminate seeds. Add salt, and sugar if required.

Refrigerate until ready to serve.

AHEAD-OF-TIME NOTES

Berry purée can be made a day in advance.

MANGO SAUCE

This is a colorful sauce that is not in the usual color schemes of most desserts.
It is a welcome addition and adds brightness. Make sure that the mango flavor complements the dessert you
serve it with; don't use it just because it looks pretty.

ABOUT 3 CUPS

3 ripe mangoes
¹/₂ cup Sugar syrup (page 239)
¹/₂ teaspoon lemon juice

Peel the mangoes and remove the flesh from the seed.

In a food processor, purée the mangoes. Strain the purée. Stir in the sugar syrup and lemon juice.

Refrigerate until ready to serve.

AHEAD-OF-TIME NOTES

The sauce can be made a day in advance.

MAPLE SYRUP SAUCE

Serve this sauce with the Banana Fritters (page 181) or the Pumpkin Soufflé (page 132), or turn the Morning Apple Cake (page 128) into an evening dessert with this sauce and Vanilla Ice Cream (page 240).

1 ½ CUPS

1 cup pure maple syrup
½ cup dark rum
1½ tablespoons freshly squeezed lime juice

In a small bowl whisk together the maple syrup, rum, and lime juice. Refrigerate until ready to serve.

AHEAD-OF-TIME NOTES

The sauce can be made a day in advance.

SUGAR SYRUP

Sugar syrup is used in recipes because it dissolves instantly. It is very easy to make.

ABOUT 1 ½ CUPS

1¼ cups granulated sugar
1 cup water

In a small saucepan, stir together the sugar and water. Over high heat bring the mixture to a boil. Boil until the sugar dissolves, about one minute.

AHEAD-OF-TIME NOTES

The sugar syrup will keep for at least 2 weeks. Store in the refrigerator.

VANILLA ICE CREAM

This recipe makes a good vanilla ice cream and can also be used as a base for many other flavors. Ice creams are an essential and delicious contribution to desserts, whether served by themselves or as an accompaniment. When serving ice cream with other desserts make sure the ice cream is a necessary part of the overall composition, or the total preparation can be too rich.

ABOUT 1 ½ QUARTS

6 large egg yolks

1 cup granulated sugar

Pinch of salt

2 cups heavy whipping cream

1½ cups milk

1 vanilla bean

Fill a medium-sized bowl ⅓ full of ice water. Set aside.

In a medium mixing bowl whisk together the egg yolks, sugar, and salt.

In a medium heavy-bottomed saucepan combine the cream and milk. Cut the vanilla bean in half lengthwise, scrape out the insides of the bean, and add the entire bean, including seeds, to the cream-milk mixture. Scald the cream mixture over medium-high heat. Slowly whisk it into the reserved egg mixture. Return the mixture to the saucepan and cook over medium heat, stirring constantly until it coats the back of a spoon, about 5 minutes.

Pour the mixture back into the mixing bowl. Place the bowl in the bowl of ice water. Stir occasionally until cool, and then strain. Refrigerate for 1 hour.

Freeze in an ice cream machine according to manufacturer's instructions.

VARIATIONS

ALMOND ICE CREAM

Off the heat, infuse 1½ cups toasted, coarsely chopped natural almonds in the hot cream mixture for 30 minutes. Strain the nuts from the cream before freezing, and discard them. Freeze the ice cream and then fold in 1½ cups of new toasted and coarsely chopped natural almonds. (It may seem like a waste to throw away the nuts and add new ones after freezing the ice cream, but the infused nuts will be soggy in the ice cream.)

CAPPUCCINO ICE CREAM

Add 3 tablespoons of ground espresso or strong coffee grounds to the cream mixture before scalding.

CHOCOLATE ICE CREAM

Whisk 6 ounces of finely chopped bittersweet chocolate into the hot cream mixture before cooking it on top of the stove.

AHEAD-OF-TIME NOTES

Ice cream bases can be made 1 to 2 days before they are frozen. Ice cream can be frozen several days in advance of when you plan to serve it. (If you make it in advance just make sure there is enough left when you need it!)

ORANGE HONEY ICE CREAM

ABOUT 1 ½ QUARTS

8 large egg yolks
¼ cup honey
¼ cup granulated sugar
Pinch of salt
2 cups milk
2¼ cups heavy whipping cream
Peel from 2 large oranges

Fill a medium mixing bowl ⅓ full of ice water. Set aside.

In a medium mixing bowl, whisk together the egg yolks, honey, sugar, and salt. Set aside.

In a medium heavy-bottomed saucepan combine the milk, cream, and orange peel. Scald the mixture over medium-high heat. Cover the saucepan and remove it from the heat. Let the orange cream steep for 20 minutes. Remove the cover and again scald the cream.

Whisk the orange cream into the reserved egg mixture; then pour it back into the saucepan. Cook the orange cream over medium-low heat, stirring constantly and making sure to scrape the bottom of the saucepan, until it coats the back of the spoon, about 5 minutes.

Pour the mixture back into the mixing bowl. Place the bowl in the bowl of ice water. Stir occasionally until cool. Strain the ice cream base through a medium sieve. Refrigerate for at least 1 hour.

Freeze in an ice cream machine according to manufacturer's instructions.

AHEAD-OF-TIME NOTES

Ice cream bases can be made a day before they are frozen. Ice cream can be frozen several days in advance of when you plan to serve it.

ACKNOWLEDGMENTS

Michael, Sara, and Michael
for visually and graphically articulating my desserts
and making the process so enjoyable

Fillamento and Sue Fisher King for their beautiful dishes

Earl Darny, Mary Curley, Dana Morgan,
Paula McShane, Angela Brassigna, Shelly Southwick, Chris Lasack,
Mimi Csolti, Lisa Moretti,
and Caroline Tsuyuki for their patience and perseverance in recipe testing

INDEX

Page numbers in *italics* refer to illustrations.